Athletes for Sale

ATHLETES FOR SALE

by Kenneth Denlinger
and Leonard Shapiro

THOMAS Y. CROWELL COMPANY
Established 1834   New York

The publisher is grateful to Macmillan Publishing Company, Inc., for permission to reprint material from *Wilt*, by Wilt Chamberlain and David Shaw, copyright © 1973 by Wilt Chamberlain and David Shaw; and to *Sports Illustrated* for permission to reprint material from "In Defense of the Competitive Urge," by Gerald R. Ford with John Underwood.

Manufactured in the United States of America

Library of Congress Cataloging in Publication Data

Denlinger, Kenneth.
    Athletes for sale.

    1. College sports. 2. Athletes—United States. I. Shapiro, Leonard, 1947–   joint author. II. Title.
GV583.D45 1975   796.3   74-32034
ISBN 0-690-00602-0

1 2 3 4 5 6 7 8 9 10

For Carol and Diane, who said yes

Acknowledgments

ABOVE ALL, to Adrian Dantley and Bruce Buckley, their families, Mrs. Virginia Dantley and Mrs. Muriel Jenkins and Mrs. Mildred Buckley, and coaches Morgan Wootten and Roy Henderson, who allowed us to enter their lives for so long and were so generous with their time and their thoughts.

To our friends in the coaching profession—among them John Thompson of Georgetown, Tom Davis of Lafayette, and Bill Wall of MacMurray—who recognized the problems in college athletics and spoke openly and honestly about them.

And particularly to Dale Brown of Louisiana State University, a basketball coach who cherishes the truth as much as he does a 6-8 blue-chipper.

To the athletes who shared their experiences, especially

Larry Wright, James Monroe, Paul Gabel, Ed Epps, Mark Cartwright, Gavin Smith, Al Green, Bernard King, Bob Whitmore, and Leon Love.

To the Washington *Post* and editors Ben Bradlee, Howard Simons, Jim Clayton, Martie Zad, Bob Levey, Don Graham, Bill Elsen, and Bill Dickinson for allocation of space and money to the project in its earliest stages.

To *Post* reporters Paul Attner, Herman Blackman, Tom Boswell, David DuPree, William Gildea, Nancy Scannell, George Solomon, and Kenneth Turan for information and encouragement.

To our colleagues around the country—especially Jeff Prugh and Dwight Chapin of the Los Angeles *Times*, Dick Weiss of the Philadelphia *Daily News*, Chan Keith of the Minneapolis *Star*, Bill Millsaps of the Richmond *Times-Dispatch*, and Dan Caughlin of the Dayton *Daily News*—for their leads and their sources.

Special thanks to Jim Bukata, who knows why; to Jacques de Spoelberch of International Literary Management, who considered the subject worthy of a book; and to Jay Acton of Crowell, the major reason it became one.

And deepest thanks and love to John and Elizabeth Denlinger and Joseph and Julia Shapiro for being our parents.

Contents

Athletes for Sale

Introduction

ON THE AFTERNOON of January 19, 1974, there unfolded an event countless sports authorities had thought only Clifford Irving could concoct. For the first time in three years and 89 games—and after an incredible Notre Dame comeback —UCLA lost a basketball game. It was the end of the most remarkable record in all of team sports, and it took shape when a freshman forward named Adrian Dantley bloodied the lip of college basketball's top player, Bill Walton.

It was no accident that Walton and Dantley performed before millions that day, and it was not entirely accidental that Dantley drew blood from Walton during an early struggle for a rebound and refused his hand after another flurry of elbows shortly before halftime. Or surprising that Walton reacted to the latter incident with a laugh and later walked to the team bus, after his first loss in 143 games, humming the Notre Dame fight song.

They were so unalike in so many ways: Walton was

1

nearly 7-foot and white, from a family of six in the San Diego suburb of La Mesa, talented enough to maintain a Garbo-like existence with the press and to have signed a multimillion-dollar, multiyear pro contract a month before graduation. Dantley was barely 6-foot-5 and black, a child of a broken home and the intense and rugged playground courts a continent away in Washington, D.C., a man-child of enormous potential but as yet relatively anonymous, an important complement to another gifted center, John Shumate.

Although they knew each other only by reputation, Walton and Dantley were bound by a symbolic thread, one that has been unwinding since man began manipulating man and has linked the Twelve Disciples and the Four Horsemen, Goliath and Moses Malone, Dwight Eisenhower and Joe Namath, Einstein and Vince Lombardi. They were all recruits. Webster defines the verb "recruit" as "to enlist (new members) for an organization," and recruiting has been practiced, in one form or another, by the Philistines and the Republicans, AT&T and Juilliard, governments and university athletic departments, anyone or any group that could become better with the addition of a well-developed mind or body, personality or hook shot.

The nation's collegiate athletic departments have managed to recruit with a special intensity that sometimes borders on the absurd and obscene. Dr. James Naismith invented basketball in 1891 and scored a recruiting coup of sorts a year later when he courted and married the best woman player, Maude Sherman. Yet he surely would be appalled by what has been done to his game.

Each year the colleges that take sports seriously send their athletic salesmen out to comb the country for the fresh talent required to maintain their prestige, pay for their stadiums and arenas, mollify their students, and pry open alumni pocketbooks.

It is an athletic maxim that a man with no special coaching skills can win games if he recruits well and that a tactician without talented players is a man soon without a job. The coaches' alphabet begins with W and ends with L.

A few of their teen-age prospects could nurse a razor blade for eight months, yet they are able to cause the likes of Bear Bryant and Lefty Driesell, Joe Paterno and Dean Smith and, yes, even The Wizard—John Wooden—more than a few uncomfortable moments. None of the players would attract 100-odd scholarship offers were it not for their postgraduate moves and jump shots, and many attract far more than the NCAA maximum of a free education and $15 per month for incidentals.

The toughest job for the coaches is not finding the proper players, for anyone who wants to know can find out easily who most of the best high school players are, but getting them to sign a document called a grant-in-aid and later an enrollment form. "Pimpish" is how the Marquette coach, Al McGuire, describes the ordeal.

Says Louisiana State University basketball coach Dale Brown: "Athletics is creating a monster. . . . Recruiting is getting to be cancerous. . . . The whole thing is sick, but nobody wants to talk about it. The NCAA has a whole bunch of damn rules but all it does is make it harder for those of us who are trying to do it honorably. It polices us, puts more of a bit in our mouths. If you're a cheater, hell, you could care less about jaywalking. If you're a murderer, do you think you could care about double parking? Well, the NCAA is worried about double parking and jaywalking when it should be cracking down on rape and assault."

If anyone close to collegiate athletics travels long enough

and far enough, he will encounter, among other kinds of hustlers, such unabashed middlemen as Freddie the Spook, who calls himself "the front man for the $300 suits," as well as for prospects and parents eager to align themselves not with the best school but the highest bidder.

The recruiting pitch varies. Some schools sell an education ("Ma'am, this is what the boy is coming for, naturally"), and some require merely that the athlete be able to throw a football, not autograph it.

One coach tells of a track man, barely literate, who pondered what to put in the space marked "race or nationality" on his college admissions application. Finally he scrawled: "440-yard dash." On the multiple-choice College Board tests, one Washington-area basketball player chose the letter *c* and used it for every answer, because he figured he could do no better by reading the questions. Reportedly, both the track man and the basketball player received some scholarship offers.

When Bob Cousy was head coach at Boston College, he received a phone call once from a man who identified himself as the high school adviser of a player named David (Big Daddy) Lattin, who was interested in attending BC.

"How are his grades?" Cousy wondered.

"He's a B student," the adviser said.

"How did he do on the Boards?" Cousy asked.

There was silence on the other end of the line, then some muffled talk, then the adviser replying: "Big Daddy says he sweeps 'em at both ends of the court." Lattin later was one of the dominant players on a Texas Western team that won the NCAA title in 1966.

"There are more liars and hypocrites than amateurs made through the efforts of colleges to keep within the boundaries of the conference rules," said Illinois football coach George

Huff. He said it in 1905, so the excesses and abuses of college sports recruiting have not been delivered by the jet age, only made easier and more widespread.

In his autobiography, Wilt Chamberlain wrote: "The big rumor in those days [the mid-'50s] was that wealthy Kansas Alums had put up a $30,000 slush fund to be turned over to me when I graduated, and the NCAA asked me a lot about that. I told them, quite honestly, that just wasn't true. And it wasn't. The figure was probably less than $20,000. And it wasn't a slush fund. The arrangement was that once I was a sophomore, playing for the varsity, I'd get spending money whenever I needed it. No specific sums were mentioned. That's why I was able to tell the NCAA what I did. The alums gave me a few names and said, 'Go see these guys when you need a few bucks.'

"I rarely had to ask for anything, though. The team won so many games and I scored so many points, they were always coming up to see me afterward and shoving wads of bills into my hands or my pockets. It might be $5 or $10 or $100, and it just kept coming. I guess I got about $15,000 or $20,000 while I was there, but I really don't know for sure; I never kept any records.

"How did I justify taking the money? Well, in the first place, just about every other top star was being taken care of; why not me? I needed the money more than the guys who gave it to me, anyway. Besides I was getting much less from Kansas than I could've gotten at almost any of the other big schools that tried to recruit me. But the main reason I took the money was pure economics: With me playing basketball, Kansas University, the city of Lawrence, the state of Kansas, and all of these alums got richer. People bought clothes and rented motels while they were there. The publicity attendant on my play brought even more money to Kansas, both directly and indirectly. Why should I let them exploit me, without reaping at least a little bit of the profit myself?"

Precisely. What do you do when you are young and hungry and someone slips you $10 or $20 or sends you shoes or a suit of clothes through the mail, even though you and everyone else know it is against the rules?

Or what is your reaction if an arena is half-filled now but will be overflowing a year or two from now mainly because of your skills, and the school figures to reap tens of thousands of dollars in additional television and tournament money—and all they can offer is a free education and $15 a month? Wilt Chamberlain said he took the money—with no guilt pangs. He was neither the first collegiate athlete to do it nor the last.

There is recruiting, in varying degrees, in every collegiate sport, from crew to girls' basketball, from the Houston golf dynasty that began with Rex Baxter in the mid-'50s to Southern California importing sprinters and jumpers from Jamaica, and Villanova luring middle-distance runners from Ireland. Much of it is honorable and aboveboard, a healthy experience that broadens a young man's view of himself and his environment. It can lead to marvelous, lasting friendships, and be the path to a more comfortable life. It led one young man to the presidency.

"In 1931, when I was being recruited out of South High in Grand Rapids (Michigan), Harry Kipke himself, the famous Michigan coach, brought me to Ann Arbor for a visit," wrote President Gerald R. Ford for *Sports Illustrated.* "I had made two all-state teams—one of which I captained —and must have been worth rushing because Michigan State, Northwestern and Harvard also expressed interest, and in those days recruiting wasn't as widespread as it is today.

"The Kipkes took me to their home for the weekend, and to several sports events, and then to the bus on Sunday night. I had to be impressed by the personal attention.

"So the hotshot center from Grand Rapids came to live at Michigan, in a third-floor 10-by-10 room way in the back of the cheapest rooming house I could find. I shared the rent ($4 a week) with a basketball player from my hometown. We each had a desk and a bed, which pretty much exhausted the floor space, and there was one small window between us.

"The Big Ten did not give athletic scholarships then. My tuition was paid by a scholarship from South High, and Coach Kipke got me a job waiting on tables in the interns' dining room at University Hospital and cleaning up the nurses' cafeteria. My aunt and uncle sent me $2 a week for Depression-day extravagances. My father's paint factory was going through a depression of its own, and since there were three other Fords to raise he couldn't send anything.

"When I pledged Delta Kappa Epsilon my sophomore year, I moved into the fraternity house and got a job washing dishes. There were four of us at the sink. . . . As dishwashers I would say we showed good early foot but uncertain technique. I doubt we would pass today's sanitation codes."

But recruiting is foul enough now for the NCAA to have increased its enforcement staff elevenfold—to 12—in the last five years, and for the University of Michigan athletic director, Don Canham, to say: "Recruiting is worse now than it used to be because it's not just the coach's job, it's the whole damn program that's going down the drain." And a host of administrators throughout the country are publicly hoping "it doesn't take another scandal to clean things up."

At its worst, recruiting bloats the self-esteem of the young athletes and encourages the notion that they are superior not only to their peers but also to the rules of their games and their society. A practice that may have the opposite effect on self-image, and is almost as bad as the under-the-table abuses, slush funds, and false promises is the stockpiling of talent by some schools at an astonishing rate. For every Bill Walton and Joe Namath there is someone gathering splinters who could be playing regularly for another school.

But even if the several dozen basketball players, several hundred football players, and scattered runners, jumpers, and hitters about the country capable of altering a college program drastically by themselves made it perfectly clear at the outset that they would bend no rules, the pressures still would be terrific.

Imagine, if you will, being young and still reasonably naive and being hustled by the best and brightest of the nation's coaches. How do you say no when the pitchmen are John Wooden and Lefty Driesell, Bear Bryant and Joe Paterno?

Ultimately, the responsibility lies with each university and its chief executive officer, who determine the size and the tone of the athletic program.

"[But] how can a president constantly monitor them [the coaches], or monitor the booster who takes a personal interest in an athlete?" said Dr. Stephen Horn, president of Long Beach State, when it was penalized in 1974 for some of the most serious recruiting violations in NCAA history. "Now it comes out. One booster told us he gave an athlete money to travel to his grandmother's funeral. But the booster began getting suspicious when she died for the third time."

In 1961 a New York University graduate student, Thomas Affinito, preparing a term paper, created a fictitious basketball player named "Tom Fini" and sent letters to 11 coaches—at schools such as Memphis State, Gonzaga, the University of Portland and Kentucky Wesleyan—saying he had been two-time all-Connecticut, was 6-foot-5 and weighed 200 pounds, averaged 23.4 points a game, and was a straight-C student.

With each letter requesting a scholarship, Affinito enclosed a phony clipping he ordered printed at the newspaper where he worked part-time and a random action photo from the paper's library. Within two weeks, two schools offered him full scholarships; one offered him a half-scholarship to be changed to full if he became a starter on the freshman team; five schools telephoned or wired within a day after he sent the letter; and four colleges sent admission forms—one with the $5 application fee crossed out.

Nearly anyone with the proper fame and influence is himself recruited by university athletic departments to help harness fresh talent, from the Kennedy brothers (Harvard) to former secretary of state Dean Rusk (Davidson), from Arnold Palmer (Wake Forest) to Henry Aaron (Georgia), from Bing Crosby (Gonzaga) to Secretariat (Kentucky).

Occasionally, a school will recruit for another school. This happened once in the early 1960s, when a quarterback from western Pennsylvania wanted to attend the University of Maryland but his College Board scores were not high enough. He took the exam again, and in late August waited anxiously in Maryland's athletic department while an assistant football coach went downstairs and brought back the letter containing the second set of scores.

The quarterback again was a few points under the 750 score required for admission. So the coach, Tommy Nugent, anxious that the quarterback not attend a school that would play Maryland in the near future, phoned his friend

Bear Bryant and sold him on the prospect. A plane ticket arrived the next day, and Joe Namath soon was on his way to Alabama.

In other years, the pressures and temptations faced by Namath and Chamberlain were also experienced by Jim Ryun, O. J. Simpson, and thousands of other gifted young men. The ordeal always is more intense with basketball players, because they have a greater individual impact on their sport. A Joe Namath or an O. J. Simpson still requires blockers to succeed. All a top basketball player needs are teammates who'll feed him the ball and clear out to let him work.

For a year we entered the lives of two exceptional basketball players, Adrian Dantley and Bruce Buckley. A good portion of this book will examine in detail how they reacted to the pressures of recruiting—how and why they chose their colleges, how their families behaved, the coaches who went after them, what tactics were used on them, and ultimately whether their decisions were wise ones. The book will also profile other players and their families, as well as some of the many coaches, alumni, and middlemen who play a part in the recruiting system, and will show how recruiting was done in the early days of college athletics, how would-be reformers have tried to clean things up in the past, and what solutions may be possible in the future.

1 / Two Blue Chippers

HE HAD JUST FINISHED the most satisfying basketball game of his life, dominating the best high school players in America, and he was about to pay the price. It began with a brief stroll across the now-empty court and out through a lobby filled with the top college coaches waiting to pump his hand, puff his ego, and clutter his already confused mind with more flattery and more promises.

"It's wide open. I haven't made up my mind and I'll listen to anyone," Adrian Dantley said. His tone was almost defiant, because he realized now—for the first time—that he would have few private moments until he offered his services to one of those eager coaches.

The Minnesota coach, Bill Musselman, was the first to grab Dantley's hand. They talked for about three minutes, the coach squinting almost directly upward at the 6-foot-5 high school senior dressed in the De Matha High jacket, inexpensive gray shirt, black slacks, and basketball shoes that had been his off-court uniform throughout this most prestigious of festivals—the Dapper Dan tournament in Pittsburgh.

The Dapper Dan annually collects a team of United States all-stars, of whom Dantley was one, and a team of Pennsylvania all-stars who have recently ended their high school careers. Several hundred recruiters are on hand to watch these gifted teen-agers—and sometimes bid for them—with the calm detachment of cattle barons judging prize steers.

In the game against the Pennsylvanians, Dantley hit 7 of 8 field-goal tries and 11 of 12 free throws, and grabbed 12 rebounds. He was a runaway choice for most valuable player, and he was the reason all the recruiters lingered in the Civic Arena lobby while the other players filtered through late on the night of March 30, 1973.

A prospect sees these coaches in a far different light than fans, students, and alumni. They seemed so very vulnerable as they waited to see the Dapper Dan stars, not at all like the forceful and determined molders of men their image makers portray. They shifted uneasily, and hoped desperately not to commit a blunder that would cause Dantley to utter that one frighteningly final word—"No."

From Musselman, Dantley moved to the Maryland delegation, four-strong and led by head coach Lefty Driesell. As with Musselman and those who were to follow, Driesell and his three assistants tried to cement a relationship that had begun months earlier.

"I hate to talk to kids like this," said the Hawaii hustler, Bruce O'Neil, waiting his turn. "But if you don't, you finish last."

Trying ever so hard to avoid last place, O'Neil stepped into Dantley's path a few seconds later, after Florida and North Carolina State had paid their respects. Hawaii was a late entry, and obviously an intriguing one. Dantley promised to pay a visit—at the school's expense—someday soon.

Then he left the lobby through a side door, with the Marquette assistant, Hank Raymond, on one arm and the mother of one of its standout players, Maurice Lucas, on the other. An hour or so later, just past midnight, Dantley had a snack with Maryland assistant Tim Autry and then sat down for another chat with Musselman that lasted well past 1 A.M.

The following day, as the bus that would take Dantley, his mother, Virginia, his aunt, Muriel Jenkins, and his cousin, Frankie, to the airport pulled to the curb outside the hotel at midmorning, North Carolina State coach Norm Sloan happened by, possibly by coincidence.

"Adrian, just a swell game last night," Sloan said, shaking Dantley's hand and suggesting he call a bit later, when things were somewhat less confused. Before the plane left the Pittsburgh airport for Washington—and home—North Carolina coach Dean Smith appeared from the first-class section. He exchanged pleasantries, then returned to his seat after saying, "Of course, I have a car waiting for us when we land."

Not long after they entered high school, in 1969, Adrian Dantley and Bruce Buckley already were being courted by the collegiate basketball elite, to influence the choices they would make by late spring in 1973.

Dantley was a product of Washington, D.C., and its intense and rugged asphalt playground courts that had been proving grounds for such as Elgin Baylor, Dave Bing, and Austin Carr.

Buckley was a child of suburban Prince George's County and an atmosphere of backyard baskets almost delicate by comparison. Both he and Dantley were raised primarily by their mothers, Buckley because his father had died 12 years before and Dantley because of a divorce.

A tall and talented Buckley on the Bladensburg High team had been a tradition for more than a decade. First there was Jay, a 6-foot-11 scholar-athlete who had the peddlers of college scholarships scurrying about their campuses in search of the physics department. He chose Duke and made academic All-America while helping the basketball team attain the final round of the NCAA tournament in 1963 and 1964.

There were fewer rules back then. Prospects were allowed unlimited expense-paid visits to a school. Now each is permitted just one.

Entertainment for players was unrestricted, so the Buckleys and their hosts kept popping up at the most fashionable places—the Blue Room of the Shoreham Hotel, for instance—and not being bashful about what they ordered. They had lunch, at their convenience, with a senator from Maryland in the Senate dining room.

During Bruce's recruitment, entertainment was limited to the campus, although the schools still trotted out their important supporters to impress the family. Ironically, Mrs. Buckley found herself treating the recruiters to an occasional snack at her home. They were forbidden to pick up the tab even for a cup of coffee, and to be seen in a restaurant was to start whispers about who paid for which ham on rye.

A young prospect from Crystal City, Missouri, named Bill Bradley was to have been a teammate of Jay's, but he soured on Duke—and recruiting—shortly after signing a grant-in-aid and switched to Princeton.

"I felt guilty about it for a long time," Bradley said after taking advantage of a Rhodes scholarship and playing professionally with the New York Knicks. "Then I matured and realized the real guilty party was them, not me. It was the same old story with me, grown men taking advantage of an 18-year-old kid."

Except for the pushy types who keep hearing no as maybe, Mrs. Buckley says she did not have a recruiting experience she would call depressing. Hectic, but never nasty.

"There was a time when the only long-distance calls we got were for marriages and deaths in the family," she says. "When the recruiting began, two or three each day became ordinary."

In 1959 she welcomed Duke coach Vic Bubas and his young aide, Bucky Waters, then sporting a fashionable flat-top haircut, and the Maryland head coach, Bud Millikan, and the energetic Lefty Driesell, who had recently switched from selling encyclopedias to selling Davidson.

One of Jay's first trips beyond the county line was to the University of Michigan, and he was wearing a new blue suit for the occasion. A straight-arrow of the highest order, he found himself on the plane sitting next to a man who immediately ordered cocktails, which was all right until the plane suddenly lurched downward several hundred feet and the drinks drenched his new clothes. He met the men of Michigan reeking of whiskey.

But not all high school athletic standouts dream of college athletic glory, as the next talented Buckley, David, was to prove. He was much smaller than Jay, 6-foot-3, but much more coordinated, and the peddlers treated him affectionately until he decided architecture was more important than basketball.

This collision between academics and athletics had been building in David since the second grade. When he made his choice, Mrs. Buckley, financial director for the Prince

George's County library system, paid his way to the University of Virginia. David has played basketball only casually ever since.

Now Bruce, the final Buckley, had grown up in this unusual blend of academics and athletics. He was nearly as tall as Jay, 6-foot-8, and nearly as coordinated as David. He had received three B's since junior high, but nothing less than A as a final grade.

In the ninth grade Buckley received the typical first overture from the peddlers, a form letter from Driesell asking him to fill out an enclosed questionnaire. Oh, yes, the letter added, would you please list some of the good players you've played against?

Before his senior season, Bladensburg's coach, Roy Henderson, arranged for Buckley and his pursuers to meet in a vacant classroom during a free period near the end of the day. Most of them were young assistants, eager to mold a relationship for the head coach to cement later.

Usually several coaches would visit each week, with three of them sometimes dropping by in one day. North Carolina sent all of its assistants and also postcards from the Rainbow Classic in Hawaii. Dean Smith flew up in a private plane to watch one of Buckley's practices.

As Buckley honed his skills and Bladensburg eventually won the Maryland state championship his senior year, the letters and interest increased. As a courtesy, he and his mother once sat down and composed polite rejection letters to 101 schools.

Buckley was frail compared with many prospects—Dantley especially. But most of the doubters about his ability to work effectively near the basket in major-college competition were converted by an excellent 1972 summer-league game against another All-Metropolitan, Larry Herron of

Mackin High, and 1973 post-season all-star games against most of the best Washington-area seniors.

Buckley had exceptional shooting range for a tall player, but the major-college coaches were gambling on his gaining weight and strength and on the fact that his competition was not always the best.

For Dantley, like so many before him, the grip of sports had been mysteriously tight. It began long ago, with his tossing sponge balls through the transom at his home. He had a brief affair with football before developing a passion for basketball that would one day cause him to remark of his pending collegiate social life: "I need social life, but I want to be happy. If I'm averaging 15 points a game as a freshman, I'll be satisfied. Social life don't mean that much because I love basketball."

It was not until the ninth grade, when he became a starter in one of the most envied basketball programs in the country—De Matha High of Hyattsville, Maryland—that Dantley began to sense that all the work was finally beginning to pay dividends.

Friends recall the pre–De Matha Dantley as a fatty, who kept in some semblance of shape by running from one McDonald's in Washington to the next. Even now he has a weight problem.

One Christmas he was nibbling on a pecan roll, then another, and another, and mumbling, "It's up to him."

"Up to who?" asked his mother.

"Up to the college coach to get me in shape."

It was a rare day when Dantley was not perfecting all the moves and sly tricks, the holds and tugs that would serve him so well in the future. He always was willing and able to throw his weight around.

Ed Epps, a recent All-Met from Washington's Cardozo High, was flexing his skills before entering Indian River Junior College in Florida when he first went one-on-one against Dantley. "He was wearing a George Washington U. sweatshirt and doing well enough so I figured he was at least a sophomore in college," says Epps. "He just wore me out. He was beating on me when *he* had the ball. I asked the guys about him and they said, 'That's Adrian Dantley, he's in the ninth grade.' "

James Brown of Harvard, who helped Dantley into the playground system and out of a scrape or two, delights in telling how his close friend almost destroyed Bud Stallworth one summer. In a pickup game at the University of Maryland, Dantley took Stallworth inside, worked him over grandly, and scored nearly every time he got the ball. Stallworth was an All-America at Kansas and No. 1 choice of the Seattle SuperSonics at the time. Dantley was not quite a senior in high school.

Still, Dantley often had hard lessons to learn, because he was playing postgraduate basketball at a tender age, with instructors like Austin Carr, Sid Catlett, James Brown, Epps, and Kermit Washington, later the top draft choice of the Los Angeles Lakers after averaging 20 points and 20 rebounds for his three-year career at American University.

When Dantley was an eighth-grader at Backus Junior High, De Matha coach Morgan Wootten—one of the most successful and envied high school coaches in the country— was more interested in coaxing a teammate, Eugene Robinson, to his school. Because James Brown played for De Matha, a private Catholic school, Dantley quietly enrolled —and it was not long before many besides the coach recognized his unlimited potential.

Dantley, nearly as tall then as he is now, came off the bench as a freshman in the season opener for De Matha, hit his first four shots, and scored 15 points. He was a starter two games later. Like Buckley, whom he knew only casually, Dantley was burdened with the weight of stardom. But his was more intense.

Dantley admits to a sensitive set of ears. When the opposition on the court was unable to divert his attention from the job at hand, the opposition in the stands sometimes could. He has been known to exchange words with fans and offer at least one challenge that went unaccepted.

Part of the reason Dantley was not universally admired was his playing style. He asked no quarter and gave none. Another reason was a smile that sometimes came off as a sneer and confidence that some interpreted as arrogance. "I don't think anyone can handle me one-on-one," he said after the Dapper Dan tournament.

After a De Matha–Mackin game early his senior season, Dantley was walking in the parking lot when a gang hurled a threat he could not ignore. "I charged one of them," he said later. "That's when all of them came at me. Then some of my friends helped me. I'm not sure what would have happened if it hadn't been for my friends."

Before the De Matha–Mackin rematch, Dantley received several telephone threats. The game was rough and close, with Dantley jeering the officials, Larry Herron, and the crowd every now and then, gliding up and down the court with that wolfish grin, and scoring at all the appropriate times. There were no incidents and De Matha won when its worst shooter popped in a 30-footer at the buzzer.

Still, Dantley constantly seemed to have to prove his skills, especially to himself. It was he more than any other De Matha player who looked most often to Morgan Wootten on the bench.

"I want him to play for a man like Morgan, or a better one if that's possible," said Mrs. Dantley, grateful to

Wootten for shielding her and her son whenever possible.

When Wootten, who compiled a 475-64 record his first 17 years of high school coaching, was confident of a De Matha victory, he sometimes moved Dantley to wing, his probable position in college. When there was any doubt about the outcome, Dantley was inside near the basket.

Mount St. Mary's offered Dantley his first full-ride scholarship, when he was a freshman at De Matha, then got in line with more than 250 other colleges.

During his four years at De Matha, Dantley scored more than 2,500 points, maintained a C-plus average, and was selected All-Metropolitan three times. He was the object of a story in *Newsweek* and two television specials.

He was the most valuable player in the most prestigious high school tournament in the country—in fact the most valuable player in nearly every tournament he played—yet he was having an agonizing time making the seemingly uncomplicated choice of a college, because it seemed as though half the country wanted to help.

2 / The Illustrious Early History of Recruiting

"By 1919, there began to spread through the East and South and along the Pacific Coast a contagion of ready assistance to promising athletes, which was initiated and coordinated by older hands. The result is that today, notwithstanding many statements to the contrary, the colleges and universities of the United States are confronted with acute problems of recruiting and subsidizing." [1]

The above quote is from a study of American collegiate athletics by the Carnegie Foundation for the Advancement of Teaching, but it is not something recently conceived and now awaiting action by the NCAA or some Senate select committee. By "today," the conclusion in fact refers to a year—1929.

[1] Howard J. Savage, *American College Athletics* (New York: The Carnegie Foundation for the Advancement of Teaching, Bulletin 23, 1929). Throughout the chapter, this will be referred to as the Carnegie study.

It is uncertain who deserves the title of father of American collegiate sports recruiting, although the patron saints of John Wooden and Bear Bryant undoubtedly were active in the 1890s and early 1900s, when it became obvious that people were willing to pay to watch intercollegiate games, often as much as $1.50 per football match.

"The soliciting of impecunious but skilled athletes, especially football players, in the '90s was conducted openly by captains or managers," the Carnegie study said. "At least, little successful attempt was made to conceal it. Apparently, there were comparatively few direct offers of money, but nominal employment, promises of social favor and athletic success, and the allurements of college life, dangled before the naive recruit, seemed to have been more powerful in their attraction.

"The practice of dressing up the butcher's boy, the iron molder, the boiler maker, or even a bond salesman, in football clothing, which in those days concealed from partisans and opponents alike almost every distinguishing feature, was more than merely scandalous. . . . Probably this abuse was less prevalent at the great universities. At less widely known institutions, which by the lights of the time seemed to have all to gain and nothing to lose, it was flagrant. Such dishonesty was practiced as much by undergraduates as by coaches or trainers or alumni."

In a series called "Buying Football Victories," in its November and December issues of 1905, *Collier's* reported that Walter Eckersall, Amos Alonzo Stagg's All-America quarterback, enrolled at Chicago three credits short of the entrance requirements. His teammate, Leo Detray, a halfback, entered the school before he had graduated from Chicago North Division High School. Walter Steffen, an end, said he chose the University of Chicago and spurned offers from Wisconsin and Northwestern because they "haven't got the money. I tell you Chicago won't get me there for what they gave Detray," Steffen said. "I know what he got."

The head football coach at the University of Illinois admitted that his players weren't showing up at their paid university jobs, the series said. "I never yet got one a job that did his work," coach George Huff added.

In addition, the University of Minnesota paid two players outright to play in a single game (against Nebraska in 1905) and a prominent Minneapolis alumnus hired a teamster to play for the school. A quarterback and end, also from Minnesota, admitted shaving points during the 1903 Beloit game.

And the president of Stanford, in 1905, proposed the following: "Let the football team become frankly professional. Cast off all deception. Get the best professional coach. Pay him well and let him have the best men the town and the alumni will pay for. Let the teams struggle in perfectly honest warfare, known for what it is, and with no masquerade of amateurism or academic ideals. The evil in current football rests not in the hired men, but in academic lying and in the falsification of our own standards as associations of scholars and of men of honor."

Such apparent widespread abuse in the early decades of the 1900s had other thoughtful observers questioning the intent of administrations "seeking to promote scholarship and research in the graduate school" also being "responsible for the stadiums, the paid coach, and the gate receipts in the college."

"How far can an agency, whose function is intellectual, go in the development of other causes without danger to its primary purpose?" said Henry S. Pritchett in the Carnegie study. "Can a university teach equally well philosophy and salesmanship? Can it both sponsor genuine education and at the same time train raw recruits for minor vocations? Can it concentrate its attention on securing teams that win, without impairing the sincerity and vigor of its intellectual purpose? It is to these questions that the thoughtful man is finally led if he seeks to reconcile the divergent activities of the present-day American university."

The Carnegie study called the recruiting and subsidizing of athletes "the deepest shadow that darkens American college and school athletics. Probably portions of the picture are even blacker than they have been painted." And that pre-1930 picture was a dark one. To wit:

"Twenty athletes are regularly employed for the tasks that some of them estimate would engage half that number of non-athletes (Oklahoma). One superintendent of buildings (Oregon Agricultural) holds athletic workers strictly to the hours of employment, 6 to 8 A.M., but employs a regular force of janitors in addition. The payroll for these athletes is labeled 'football help.' In an extreme case, thirty-two athletes and prospective athletes were employed to maintain a small playing field and do odd jobs (New York University).

"Although it is not nowadays customary for an institution to loan money officially to athletes as such, vestiges of such practices in past years have been found (Southern California). . . . Unfortunately, it appears that the notes of athletes are collectible in comparatively few instances, even when the loan fund is administered through a local bank in order to create a sense of responsibility on the part of the athlete-borrowers.

"The practice of 'caring for' a more or less definite number of athletes, ranging from twenty-five to fifty (Bucknell, Gettysburg, Muhlenberg, Oglethorpe, Pennsylvania State, Pittsburgh, West Virginia Wesleyan), is a somewhat less formal matter than the award of athletic scholarships. Its excuse is the competitive bids of rivals, and its limit is usually 'all college expenses.' Sometimes (Boston College, Holy Cross, Notre Dame) no definite promises are made; the athlete is merely assured that he will be 'cared for.'

"Alumni subsidies are dispensed, sometimes by a member of the athletic staff or someone intimately connected with athletics, from a 'slush fund' or 'black box fund,' and thus a close supervision of beneficiaries can be maintained. . . . The amounts available in slush funds vary (Carnegie Institute of Technology, $13,000; Centre, $600; Grove City, $8,000; Lafayette, $3,000) with the interest of contributors. In an extreme case of subsidizing, alumni and businessmen made contributions ranging from $10 to nearly $1,000 annually to a fund aggregating from $25,000 to $50,000 a year. From this the college expenses of all football players were paid and additional sums, termed 'pay checks,' were disbursed to leading performers (Washington and Jefferson).

"A further consideration respecting academic standing as a factor in the support of athletes touches upon the average of grades required as a qualification for financial assistance. Of seven institutions (Baylor, Columbia, Des Moines, Rutgers, Southern California, Southern Methodist, Stanford), at which a minimum academic requirement, usually an average of C, is prescribed for the award of certain scholarships, it was approached at only two.

"The value of complimentary tickets as subsidies in kind is illustrated by the fact that a football player at a university on the Pacific Coast sold his allotment at a profit of about $100 each for various major games of a single season.

"Assistance to needy athletes at Catholic institutions takes several forms. It may be distributed as scholarships from athletic funds, covering wholly or partly tuition, board, and room in addition to assistance from individual alumni (Fordham); or jobs that provide tuition, board, and room in return for very nominal services (Notre Dame); or an outright allocation of funds without return except in athletic participation (Georgetown). Occasionally, the attempt is made to balance awards to athletes with those to non-athletes (Holy Cross). Or priests may effect arrangements among their own parishioners, members of the faculty or friends of their college by which athletes may be maintained (Boston College).

"At one university (Southern California) alumni supply fraternities with tickets to football or other contests on the understanding that the fraternities will entertain prospective athletes whom alumni have invited to visit the campus. In several cases it was clear that alumni had practically forced fraternities to entertain prospective athletes.

"Incidentally, it was once the custom of an individual alumnus to operate a kind of recruiting excursion—several special Pullman cars hired at his own expense to take athletes from the city of his residence to the campus of his university (Indiana). Three instances were encountered in which recruiting activities were being conducted by alumni apparently in opposition to the wishes of the responsible athletic authorities (Amherst, Princeton, Tennessee)."

Charlie Black remembers sitting in the Sigma Alpha Epsilon house at Kansas University in 1920 awaiting the job he had been promised in exchange for his basketball talents. He had come all the way from Alton, Illinois, and was becoming increasingly depressed.

"I'd been there two days and hadn't even met the coach [the late Phog Allen]," he said. "Then I got a telegram from Northwestern that said: 'If you come back [we'll] meet you at the train. Financial aid guaranteed.' Two hours later I had my job at KU."

For 35 cents an hour, about a dime above the going rate for labor then, Black kept the KU shower and supply rooms in order and still managed to become an All-America in 1923 and college player of the year the next season.

By 1929 Allen was moving swiftly toward becoming a legend in basketball history, and a young whiz named Bill Johnson, from Oklahoma City, could hardly resist his pitch.

"His [Allen's] son had died in a swimming accident the summer before he was to become eligible," Johnson said, "and Phog told my folks he wanted me to come up there and join his family to live as part of his family and become part of the KU plan. That pretty well convinced my family."

For the next two years, Johnson lived in the Allen attic in Lawrence, Kansas, cooked breakfast for the family each morning, and cleaned the dishes, helped install bleachers, painted and did odd jobs after classes, and cleaned up the evening dishes at the Allen household after basketball practice.

"There was no coddling," Johnson said. There was an investigation, though, just before he became eligible as a sophomore in 1930. For obvious reasons, the University of Oklahoma was upset at losing one of its natives to Allen and demanded an investigation into Johnson's "deal" at Kansas.

"After everything was presented, they said, 'This kid needs a trophy,'" Johnson said. "I earned everything I got."

Johnson, who later lived in the Phi Delt house and with a professor at KU, had a roommate in that nippy Allen attic for a few months, "a guy from back East whose name I don't recall."

Whether that young man also reminded Allen of his late son was not determined. But he was unable to adjust to the family, Johnson said, "and he didn't develop too much on the court, either."

In 1926, the first 7-footer anyone dressed in a basketball uniform, (High) Harry Kersenbrock, found his way to Kansas after playing for Doane College in Crete, Nebraska. Kersenbrock played freshman ball at KU, so well that Allen designed his entire offense and defense around him. Allen also should have locked High Harry in his attic instead of allowing him to go back home for the summer.

While paddling a canoe across the Little Blue River, Kersenbrock stood up to remove his jacket, fell overboard, and drowned. Kansas was 2-15 in 1928–29, the next season, but, by school decree, every student learned to swim. KU's next 7-footer was Wilt Chamberlain some 30 years later.

Athletes often were herded into the National Guard back in the 1920s, according to Black, because they could earn $5 by attending the weekly meetings. As a coach, Black said he only made one recruiting trip, in 1927 or '28, after Notre Dame's Knute Rockne pointed out the top 100 Nebraska high school athletes by paying their expenses to a dinner in Omaha.

"There always were a lot of rumors," said Black, now retired and living in Sacramento, California. "You'd hear how this guy was going into the athletic department and picking up his weekly $50." Players also could turn a tidy profit on tickets even then.

"But recruiting seems to be getting more vicious now," he said. "You have California boys going to play in New York and New York boys coming out to play here." Then he laughed. "If I seem mad, maybe it's because I didn't get paid enough," he said. "I didn't get a chance at that gravy."

Interestingly, the Carnegie study insists that "no single factor has contributed more directly to the use of athletic scholarships in American colleges and universities than the second qualification set by the will of Cecil Rhodes for recipients of the Oxford scholarships that bear his name." Authorized in 1902, that key second stipulation said that regard should be given to a student's "fondness for and success in manly outdoor sports, such as cricket, football and the like."

Recruiters immediately began trying to convince administrators to award aid on a more "all-around" basis, and such Rhodes scholarship winners as Supreme Court Justice Byron (Whizzer) White of Colorado, Bill Bradley of Princeton, and Tom McMillen of Maryland have distinguished themselves and their schools. However, 70 years after the awards were begun, something of their significance had been lost for at least one prospective scholar.

According to the Utah basketball coach, Jerry Pimm, a player he was talking with said he wanted "some of that highway money."

"Highway aid?" the coach said. "What do you mean?"

"You know," the player said. "I want what that guy Bradley got, one of them Rhodes scholarships."

In 1929 the Carnegie study said: "The fundamental causes of the defects of American college athletics are two: commercialism and a negligent attitude toward the educational opportunity for which the college exists. To one, and generally to both, of these inter-acting causes, every shortcoming of college sport can be traced. Both may be abated, even if neither, in view of the imperfectibility of human nature, can ever be absolutely eliminated. . . .

"The argument that commercialism in college athletics is merely a reflection of the commercialism of modern life is specious. It is not the affair of the college or the university to reflect modern life. If the university is to be a socializing agency worthy of the name, it must endeavor to ameliorate the conditions of existence, spiritual as well as physical, and to train the men and women who shall lead the nations out of the bondage of these conditions."

At the turn of the century, amateur athletics was nearly always an exercise limited to the wealthy, even though many of the best athletes were from the lower and middle classes. The compromise after the Carnegie study simply was to sanction rules of amateurism that in fact made the athletes semiprofessionals, but at least enabled them to attend the college of their choice looking slightly less like Hessians.

As the years passed, college athletics became vastly more commercial, because of television in part and also because contributions by alumni tend to reflect the won-lost record of the football team.

In 1966, when Ohio State's football team went from a 7-2 record to 4-5, alumni contributions dropped by nearly $500,000. Missouri went from a 6-5 football record and $227,409 in alumni contributions in 1959 to a 10-1 record and $442,445 in gifts a year later. Similar contrasts are true of many small-college programs.

The more than four decades since the Carnegie study have caused observers of collegiate athletics to ponder more complex questions. Is amateurism consistent with the principle of equality of opportunity? If all scholarships, academic and athletic, are based on need, it means that athletes will have to pay their tuition if they are financially able to do so, regardless of their contributions to the school. Is this fair?

Some athletes generate 10 and 20 times as much income as their scholarship is worth to a school; a very few, with Bill Walton clearly one, generate perhaps 100 times what they receive. Why not pay them their worth? The benefit to the college often goes far beyond the athlete's collegiate life. The pro football player usually trots onto the field with someone announcing his name and his college ("From Southern California, O. J. Simpson. . . . From Duke, Sonny Jurgensen") to thousands in the stands and millions over television.

Indeed, many athletes never graduate from college, and some keep both scholarship and eligibility without a C average. But if MIT chooses to produce engineers—and recruit teachers and scholars toward that end—why shouldn't Ohio State be a proper training ground for the NFL and Maryland for the NBA?

Every decade or so the rule bending gets woefully out of hand. In 1945 five Brooklyn College players admitted accepting bribes to throw a basketball game with the University of Akron. Frank Hogan, the district attorney of New York City, later reported evidence that between 1947 and 1950 a total of 86 basketball games had been fixed at Madison Square Garden and at arenas in 22 other cities by 32 players on several teams. In March 1961 Hogan disclosed another scandal that involved 37 players from 22 major colleges who accepted bribes ranging from $700 to $4,450 to fix games. The army and air force academies each have been jolted by widespread classroom cheating by football players.

To its credit, the NCAA has tried to deal with the complexities of collegiate athletics with numerous well-intentioned rules. But the recruiters, forced by pressures anyone in any other business would understand, have shown most of them to be unworkable or impractical. And sports, aided by improved air travel and television, took another huge jump toward business in the 1950s, the decade when more and more players began choosing colleges farther and farther from their hometowns.

"No prospect is more than four and a half hours from your campus by jet today," says former Oklahoma coach

Bud Wilkinson, "and the trend is to go after the super-prospect regardless of where he is from. When I was at Oklahoma, we began with a recruiting budget of $3,000, and I don't think we ever had more than $7,500. Now, that wouldn't pay your phone bill."

In 1974, eleven years after Wilkinson's last season at Oklahoma, coach Barry Switzer admitted that the Sooners incurred about $10,000 in recruiting-related expenses before signing one halfback from Miami, Florida, the gifted Elvis Peacock.

Television has been even more significant in helping the 50 superpowers in football and basketball.

"TV money is distributed equally, but exposure isn't," says the NCAA's Walter Byers. "TV tends to create an aristocracy, a super-hierarchy of teams." And that aristocracy was the major reason for the NCAA to split into three divisions in 1973.

The first telecast of a sports event in the United States was of a baseball game between Columbia and Princeton in May 1939. In 1972 and 1973, according to the NCAA, "participating members" received $13,490,000 in television rights. The 1975–76 television plan was sold to ABC-TV for $16,000,000.

In addition, the NCAA pointed out that the second Rose Bowl game, in 1916—the first one with a cash payoff—produced for the two participants, Brown and Washington State, $7,631.50, whereas "Bowl loot" from ten games in 1972 generated $7,489,271.

"UCLA has an edge in basketball today that Notre Dame never had in its football glory days," Byers insists. "Kids all over the country see coach Johnny Wooden on the tube year after year—and he's recognizable."

Jeff Prugh of the Los Angeles *Times* revealed the first

"space age" way to solve the dilemma of recruiting in 1972 when he reported that 7-foot Ralph Drollinger, from suburban San Diego, gathered facts about each school and fed them into a computer. The answer? UCLA.

There were no such advantages for Jackie Moreland, a Louisiana farm boy and honor student hustled by hundreds of schools and called "the greatest basketball prospect in the country" in 1955.

Moreland signed with North Carolina State but never played there because his name was linked with recruiting violations for which State was severely punished. He went to Louisiana Tech and later had an undistinguished career in the NBA and ABA. At 33 he died of cancer, remembered mostly as one of the foremost victims of recruiting, with his father being quoted as saying, "I don't think I'll ever raise another of my boys to be an athlete."

Not surprisingly, it has been only in the last decade that the black athlete has been recruited heavily. Even now, whether the circumstances warrant it or not, there is a tendency for recruiters to offer money more quickly to a black athlete than a white.

A study by Skip Myslenski of Knight Newspapers revealed that Texas had no black football players in 1963 and six a decade later, that Mississippi went from zero to five, Pittsburgh from two to 31, Oklahoma from zero to 22, Alabama from zero to 13, Auburn from zero to four, and Nebraska from eight to 15. Michigan State remained relatively constant at about one-third black.

"Let's face it," Texas coach Darrell Royal says. "It's a fact that when I first came to Texas [1957] it wasn't integrated. Then that changed to where the regents said we should start integrating, but meant that we really didn't have to push it, to worry about it. Then to where it was all right, they meant it. Then to gawl-dog, let's really go out and make the effort to totally integrate the school, totally integrate athletics.

"Part of it was legislation and part of it was people stopping and analyzing the situation, facing up to what is right and wrong. The laws made people do this. Oh, yes, you're right, you can't legislate what comes out of people's minds and people's hearts. But any fair-minded person who looked at it, who did some thinking about it wanted to do what was right."

Penn State enjoys a reputation as one of the most open and aboveboard schools in the country. Yet several former football players discovered State abiding by merely the letter of the rules for athletic scholarships.

State players signed the usual contract calling for them to receive "room, board, books, fees, tuition" and "$15 a month for incidentals" and stipulating that the scholarship could not be withdrawn except "through academic failure or disciplinary action."

However, the players soon learned that the $15 per month was withheld if they failed to maintain a C average, despite being eligible for football. In addition, the books—most of them used—were loaned to the players rather than given to them and could be kept after the semester only if the players paid for them.

State coach Joe Paterno insists the withholding of the $15 per month stopped "two or three years ago. It originally was an incentive not just to be eligible but to do better. It was especially good 14 or 15 years ago as an incentive to do better than average work, to get a good base as a freshman."

An NCAA official has said such incentives are against the rules. Paterno says he thought it was against NCAA rules to buy players books. According to the NCAA official, it certainly is not, as long as the school does not give the athletes the cash to buy the books.

In addition, it was implied that State would provide supplies such as pencils, paper, notebooks, and pens and that the training table would be available daily throughout the year. The former promise was patently untrue and the latter was available only during the season and spring practice—and then only for dinner. In the late '60s and early '70s, State usually was playing before near-sellout crowds and annually receiving television and bowl money running into the six figures.

"What bugged me most was being belittled in front of your peers, being told in front of the team that you stink, that you're a baby, that you're a nothing," says Paul Gabel of one experience with coach Paterno, generally lauded for his compassion and progressive ideas while compiling an enviable won-lost record at State.

"I had an asthma problem, and for two years at State I took shots, paced myself, and kept everything under control. Then I stopped the shots one summer, had a bad reaction to an insect bite, and reported to camp with a lot of congestion. The doctor said he didn't know whether I'd be able to play or not.

"Still, I was in good shape otherwise but the second day of the [August] drills we were running sprints after the usual practice of two hours or so. I felt this attack coming on and I tried to pace myself, slow down instead of keeping up with everyone.

"But he [Paterno] starts screaming, 'Get it out, get the lead out, start moving,' so I pushed myself. I went beyond what I should have done and I collapsed right there on the field. When I came to, everybody was around me and I could hear Paterno yelling and screaming, 'Get up, get up, you're a baby,' you're this, you're that. My pulse went up to about 210, and that's high. The doctor had to shoot me up with depressants to get me down.

"Anyway, I felt he [Paterno] should have made an apology to me in front of the team, because that's where he did the belittling. Instead, he came up to me at the table at lunch and apologized, just to me. Then the next day in practice he did the same thing and I had another attack. I had to quit football for a year, start the shots all over again."

"I was tough on Paul; I know I was," Paterno said after Gabel had graduated. "Sometimes the guy you drive hardest is the one with so much potential. Once in a while you go too far. But what's too much for one player is not enough for another.

"I think that because my winning-is-fun attitude has gotten so much national attention a lot of people think I'm some kind of phony. I don't believe losing is like death, although if we lost 10 in a row I might wish I were dead, but I'm as competitive as anyone. I'm a driver."

Still, State and Paterno have quite a good record of producing college graduates as well as excellent football players—and Paterno has been among the leaders in calling for recruiting reforms in addition to being among the few coaches publicly realistic about college sports and their future.

"Okay, now a coach gets the boy," Paterno said. "The recruiting rat-race is over. He's been lionized, wined, dined, told how great he is and how much he is needed. Then, after the big buildup, he finds out he's just another player on the freshman team. He isn't a hero or a star anymore. He has to make the team, just like everybody else. It's a tremendous letdown and not every youngster can adjust to it. So, all of a sudden, the coach has an unhappy player. It's all so wrong."

Indeed it is. Nearly as distasteful as the under-the-table payoffs and other blatant rule violations is the fact that every college prominent in the football and basketball polls usually recruits far more talent than it needs. For every 22 football regulars there usually are more than 70 on scholarship who play sparingly. Mostly, there are twice as many scholarship bench-sitters in basketball as starters, young men who could be playing regularly at another school at another level of competition.

Paul Gabel recalls being introduced, as a prospect fresh from Peary High in Rockville, Maryland, to the Penn State varsity by Paterno. The coach called Gabel a fullback, and most of the squad laughed, because State historically gobbles up high school fullbacks—and quarterbacks—and converts them to other positions.

"You're a defensive tackle," said Mike Reid, a former high school fullback who became an All-America defensive tackle.

"No, I'm a fullback," Gabel insisted.

"Defensive tackle," Reid shot back.

Reid was not quite correct. Gabel was an offensive lineman most of his career at State. Franco Harris was the fullback.

Jim Fitzsimmons, who later transferred to Harvard, signed with Duke rather early in the recruiting race during his senior year in high school.

"I was the first one [Duke prospect] to sign," he says. "You figure if they have five scholarships they'll sign two guards, two forwards, and a center, right? Well, Duke signs three more guards. I told him [head coach Bucky Waters] I didn't think that was fair when I left." Another of those guards, Jeff Dawson, transferred to Illinois.

Gabel says that during a visit to Alabama he happened to see the Crimson Tide recruiting list. Quickly he thumbed through the pages until he reached "fullbacks." His name was there, and so were 39 others.

Mark Cartwright is more frustrated than bitter about his experience at Maryland. A 7-footer, he was led to believe he would be one of the cornerstones in a basketball dynasty, but when it became time to build he was merely a tall support.

"I really had no one to turn to for advice during recruiting," Cartwright says. "I'd ask this coach or that one, and they'd say, 'We're the best, come to my school.' Maryland said it was going to win the NCAA tournament. It never entered my mind that I wouldn't be playing."

It never does. Cartwright, like hundreds of others before and after him, had been better than his teammates through high school, and he felt certain that he could be even more successful at Maryland. There were two reasons why he was not: Tom McMillen and Len Elmore.

"All of a sudden I realized I wasn't starting, and then I wasn't playing," Cartwright said not long after quitting Maryland in 1972 (he later enrolled at Bowling Green). "The frustration came in stages. At first I tried real hard to stay with it on the bench, but when I got in the games I'd be too nervous. Then I thought I should take more of a what-the-heck attitude on the bench, but then I was too lackadaisical in the games."

It was a bit different when Dana Lewis, the first great basketball player at Oral Roberts University, decided he wanted to transfer to the nearby University of Tulsa.

"When they heard I was thinking about leaving," Lewis recalled later, "one of the vice presidents got in touch with my mother. He said he'd just talked with the Lord and that He'd said it was His will that I stay at Oral Roberts."

Preacher-president Roberts is among the most active basketball recruiters in the country, and the 6-foot-11 Lewis recalls the man not releasing him from the scholarship contract but later calling when he transferred to Tulsa.

"The team left [for the NIT, for which Lewis was not eligible] about 2 P.M. and that's right when I got the call," Lewis said. "He wanted me to have lunch with some businessman. He also said my room was ready back there anytime I wanted it.

"My family's very religious and I'd gone to one of his rallies. They flew my mother out for a visit and then me. I fell in love with the place. He told me it was going big time right then [the mid-'60s] but he was just jiving me."

Has the experience made Lewis any less religious?

"I don't put my faith in man now," he said. "I just read my Bible."

3 / Tactics

Most days Adrian Dantley picked up a stack of letters at De Matha High and tossed them all—unopened—into either of the two huge cardboard boxes he used to collect junk mail from collegiate athletic peddlers. The letter from Arnold Palmer Enterprises was appealing, though, and he opened it enthusiastically, only to discover in the first sentence that ol' Arnie, like all the others, had something to sell.

"It is always an honor for me to commend my alma mater, Wake Forest University, to outstanding student-athletes," Palmer's pitch began, and Dantley soon recognized the key phrases that countless others had used to trumpet the college of their choice.

"Few, if any, schools like it in the country . . . athletics and academics of the highest quality . . . primary mission to provide the finest education . . . unique institution . . . personal development . . . hope you will make every effort to see it for yourself."

Dantley generally resisted the celebrity approach, and Palmer's letter eventually came to rest in the cardboard box. Dantley also politely declined when the University of Minnesota suggested dinner with Senator Hubert Humphrey and when the University of Maryland wanted to arrange a chat with Governor Marvin Mandel.

"There are certain things that turn a kid on, academically, athletically, and socially," says Denny Crum, the Louisville basketball coach who earlier had helped coax the Walton Gang to UCLA. "You've got to find out as much as you can about the boy, his family, his girl friend, his coach—everything."

Letters and telegrams, cards for every occasion, and plenty of sweet talk are recruiting staples.

A 1974 survey by the National Association of Basketball Coaches said that one of every eight major colleges made illegal offers to prospects, that all the cheaters were offering money, 80 per cent were offering cars, and more than half were offering clothing. The survey was conducted among 25 recently graduated college players, 25 current high school standouts, 25 sets of parents, and 25 athletic directors of major-college basketball programs. Of the 50 players interviewed, 40 per cent said they had received illegal offers.

"You'd say something like 'Hey, that's a nice suit' or 'That's a nice pair of shoes' and sure enough they'd arrive in the mail in a few days," says Ed Epps, former All-Metropolitan from Cardozo High in Washington, D.C., in the mid-'60s, who attended Indian River Junior College and later played at Utah State.

Epps says he and another All-Met, Harold Fox, once

were taken to a clothes warehouse with instructions to "take all you can carry, boys." They did.

"I could count on $50 and clothes if I pushed on just about every visit," he says. "If I didn't get hard cash on a trip, I'd get something later in the mail—maybe a pair of shoes or a suit or something. They know how much a black kid from the ghetto wants that money."

The all-important phrase among the coaches who bend the rules is "We'll take care of you." Sometimes it is followed by a wink.

"When you're poor, you know what that means," says a former Washington All-Met who attended a Big Ten school. "My mother had never seen anyone interested in me before and they promised her money and cars, that kind of thing. They paint a real pretty picture, and then you get thrown in the group once you get there.

"It's like, 'We got you here so we don't have to worry about you any more.' It seems like the only time they are interested in you is when you're being recruited. After it's over, there's a letdown. That's when it is that you get to realize it's nothing but a big business, who's got the most money."

Why did he choose his school?

"I liked the coach," he says. "I didn't want to go to a factory. I wanted to go to a cold climate and they made me the best offer."

In the early '50s, a line popular in football was that halfback Hugh McElhenny took a pay cut when he joined the pro San Francisco 49ers from the University of Washington. Later he was quoted as saying he "followed a trail of twenties" to Washington.

The opening strategy the collegiate peddlers used on

Dantley and Buckley was the familiar introductory letter. Dantley's first was from Bob Knight, the Indiana coach then coaching at West Point, and Buckley's was from Lefty Driesell of Maryland.

Both players were in the ninth grade, the time those with the best potential are usually solicited by the recruiters. An exception was Rick Mount, the Purdue All-America. He was being wooed by the University of Miami in the eighth grade.

Most introductory approaches are form letters describing the school and its athletic program, emphasizing the prospect's sport, and requesting that he fill out and return an athletic and academic profile. Nearly any high school player talented enough to get his name in the newspaper sports pages receives a recruiting letter, and all too often he confuses interest with a scholarship offer.

Many prospects brag that they had 75 offers when they actually had 75 letters. Maryland, for instance, might show interest in 50 basketball players each year and sign only 5 to scholarships.

"A lot of athletes concoct things," says UCLA's John Wooden. "It inflates their egos. We had a player who once told me he'd been contacted by 80 schools. I called him into the office one day and we started to talk about it. I said, 'OK, name me 80 schools, not 80 that recruited you, just 80 schools.' I think he managed about 25."

The top 40 or 50 senior basketball prospects and the top 200 or so football prospects in the country, from Maine to California and from Minnesota to Texas, are well known through a variety of scouting services.

(Duke circulated a story that one of its former centers, Mike Lewis, was recruited only after its ever-alert basketball staff received a tip from a coed who lived in Lewis' hometown in Montana. In fact, Duke had been chasing Lewis for years.)

In 1973 there were about 164,200 high school seniors playing varsity football and about 111,300 playing basketball. Of every 20 participants, though, probably only one received athletic aid to college. For the majority of those who received scholarships, including the ones given only partial aid, recruiting undoubtedly went smoothly, with the prospect and his family and the school and its coaches acting in good faith.

The rumor drifting through the Washington area about Buckley in the spring of 1973 was that North Carolina, which offered him a scholarship nine months earlier, was losing interest after he did not have a spectacular senior performance. How does a school back out on a verbal contract?

"It just stops showing interest," says one coach. "No letters, no phone calls—nothing. Usually, the kid takes the hint." A former Missouri Valley Conference assistant football coach is more specific.

"We were famous for stringing," he told Dan Coughlin of the Cleveland *Plain Dealer.* "I remember stringing one kid all the way to the end. When we got the kid we really wanted, he [the first prospect] never heard from me again. We lied to kids. We cheated to get them in school. I almost got into a fist fight with the head coach [Lee Corso] because he said we had too many black kids. I was disgusted.

"When I went to an inner-city school to talk to a black kid, I'd wear my jive clothes and talk jive. If I went to a more conservative rural school, I'd dress and talk conservatively. Some schools don't do what we did. I'd like to mention by name such schools as Purdue, Ohio State, Miami of Ohio, and Kent State who don't do what we did.

"We had two kids from Cleveland who played their last football game on a Saturday, and Monday they were flunked out of school, right in the middle of the semester. We cheated to get kids into school. The school caught one transcript that was changed."

The University of Pennsylvania permitted its black football co-captain to play for three years while he was passing only 12 of 33 subjects "in a crazy-quilt combination of sly rule bending, administrative bungling and misplaced compassion," Chuck Stone of Universal Press Syndicate reported in April 1974.

"Worse yet, the university approved Glenn Casey's playing even though he was beset with some emotional problems," Stone wrote.

Ironically, on the same weekend the Buckley rumors were at their height, North Carolina coach Dean Smith was visiting the Buckley apartment. In April, both parties were happy when Buckley signed a grant-in-aid with Carolina.

There are players, the ones whose heads seem to swell ever larger with each passing day, who take advantage of well-meaning recruiters. Many take free trips—to Louisville on Kentucky Derby weekend or to the University of Hawaii anytime—with no intention of enrolling at the school.

Lately, the phrase "Gimme a Z" is not the beginning of a cheer for a school but the requested payment by some prospects for playing collegiate basketball. The reference is to a Datsun 240Z.

Several big-time basketball schools have begun using foreign tours as an attractive pitch to prospects in addition to their value as preparation for the season. The University of North Carolina has toured Europe, North Carolina State has gone to the Orient, and Maryland has played in Mexico.

A few years before he won the NCAA basketball

tournament with North Carolina State, coach Norm Sloan was visiting an excellent prospect from the Midwest, and he says neither the player nor his parents would offer more than a few words before he took them out to dinner, this being at a time when unlimited entertainment was permitted.

At the restaurant—the gaudiest in town, of course—the player and his family suddenly were most outgoing, especially to the waiters, who they knew from similar visits financed by other schools. Later, at home, they were so aloof that Sloan never had a chance to explain the advantages of N.C. State.

But that was not quite as degrading as what arrived in his office a few days later—a form letter that said, "Dear coach, if your name is at the botton you and your school still are under consideration." Yes, Sloan's name was included, and, yes, the letter immediately was dumped into his wastebasket.

Al McGuire, the Marquette coach, says he once took a prospect and his family ("the usual six, seven people") out to dinner and asked the player if he wanted a drink. At first the player said no, but McGuire said, "Ah, come on."

The player ordered a double.

"I try to keep a certain amount of dignity," McGuire says. "I'll kiss the mother once. I'll talk to the high school coach about defense. I'll move the pepper- and salt-shakers around and that's about it. The [campus] visits drive me nuts. If it rains, I won't get the kid."

With Dantley and Buckley, there never was any doubt about four-year scholarships—not the one-year variety that became effective in August 1973. Their problems were sifting sincerity from so much sweet talk and saying no to so many persuasive men.

"So often kids tell me an assistant coach tells them

'You've just got to come to my school or I'll lose my job,' "
says the commissioner of the Atlantic Coast Conference,
Robert James. That is powerful—and certainly unreason-
able—pressure to apply to a young man. It was a major
factor in Dantley's close friend, James Brown, being
hospitalized for hypertension during his senior year at De
Matha.

"The sales pitches usually came off as pretty sincere,"
says Brown. "I was oblivious to the seedy tactics. I assumed
every recruiter had a sincere interest in me. But there were a
lot of people I couldn't say no to. I sort of brought it [the
hypertension] on myself."

One day Brown received the ultimate compliment to his
potential as a student-athlete. Side by side on coach
Morgan Wootten's desk were letters from Harvard and
UCLA. Brown eventually chose Harvard, in part because of
some low-key recruiting by Senator Edward Kennedy.

Rumors of illegal tactics and outlandish offers always are
as near as the next coach, often one who loses a prospect
and tries to rationalize it by saying "The kid went for the
money." Escrow accounts, no-work jobs, the promise of
several complimentary tickets that can be sold at ten and
twenty times their face value, "weekend women," charge
cards, cars, clothes, and that time-honored staple—hard
cash—are the most popular inducements.

"Every player is given four tickets to regular season
games and he has the option to buy four more at face
value," a former defensive lineman at a Pac-8 school said in
1974. "So you can get eight tickets and sell them at inflated
prices, usually to alumni. They buy them at those prices as a
way of supporting athletes. In 1967 we were making about
$350 a game. That's about $40 a ticket. It's sort of
institutionalized. You get your tickets and if you have [a]

contact, you sell them yourself; or if you want, the team managers will sell them for you.

"It's not always that good, though," he added. "In fact, one year—I think it was '69 when the team wasn't doing so well—the manager ended up trying to scalp the tickets and he got arrested and thrown in jail with 75 or 100 tickets. I can just imagine what the players said to him when they found out he never sold their tickets."

At the University of Washington in the mid-'60s, football starters were given four tickets to each home game and had an option to buy two more. With non-regulars, the arrangement was two free tickets and an option to buy two more. Players not suiting up had just the option to buy two tickets.

David DuPree says he made about a $2,000 profit as a three-year cornerback merely exercising the four-and-two Washington arrangement. Obviously, when a Washington player was benched, or injured seriously enough not to suit up for a home game, his pocketbook—as well as his ego or his body—was hurt.

"We'd look up and there'd be empty seats in the stands," DuPree says. "But somebody was willing to pay at least $35 a pair for tickets. I was from Seattle and my mother often wondered why I didn't invite her to the games, until I finally told her, 'Mom, it just wouldn't be financially to my advantage to have you come.' "

A favorite Atlantic Coast Conference yarn concerns one prospect who was so overwhelmed with his weekend date that he offered to pay for his own visit the next time.

Reportedly, one midwestern basketball coach brought two call girls with him while hustling a prospect at a major post-season tournament, and the four of them got along splendidly.

A junior-college player from the East was lured into a

room on some sort of flimsy academic excuse during his visit to a major college and the coaches waited—and listened—outside the door. Presently, the bed springs began to squeak, louder and more rapidly, and the head coach whispered with glee, "We got him." One college tried all of that—and more—on Larry Wright.

4 / More Fun and Games

LARRY WRIGHT, a native of Monroe, Louisiana, was the best guard in Washington, D.C., in 1973, sleek and fast and with exceptional range, the sort of player who could make a collegiate backcourt solid for four years. He still does not recall much of his first recruiting trip to one of the dozens of schools seeking his considerable talents.

Wright arrived on campus on a Friday afternoon. That night, according to his coach at Western High, Bob Piper, "they slipped him a white girl. He sent the girl out and then he called me. I told him to stay and see what else was going on." There was plenty.

He was given the customary tour of the campus on Saturday, and that night a black assistant coach escorted him to an off-campus party.

"They had this big punch bowl," Wright recalled later. "But I don't drink, and I told the coach I didn't want any. He said he wanted me to have some fun. The party was

51

supposed to be for me, so I drank a couple of cups. A few hours later I didn't know where I was. Some of the players had to help me back to the hotel room. I wasn't drunk. I've had wine before and I know what that feels like. This was something completely different.

"The next morning, I still didn't know where I was. I remember finding myself in the bathtub and not knowing how I got there." Wright managed to get on an airplane to fly home Sunday, but Piper immediately noticed "he was walking as if he was off-balance. He said he wasn't feeling good, but I thought it was just from the flight.

"The next morning we went to school. Larry couldn't make it to his first-period class. Then I took him to the doctor. From the report we got from him, Larry had some traces of drugs in his system. The way Larry described it to me, the punch was strong enough to knock a mule out. I've talked to the head coach about it, and he admitted some of their players are on drugs." Piper's next call was to the NCAA.

That same school also offered Wright a $400-per-week summer job, $50 a week during the school year, a $1,000 wardrobe at cost, a car, and six years to graduate, he said. "I'm not going to let anyone buy me," he said. "If I get a degree, I'll be able to buy a car anyway. And if you give me too much money, what do I want to kill myself playing ball for?

"I guess they figure a black kid isn't used to this kind of money, so anything they offer they think you'll jump right at it." Wright chose a scholarship offer from Grambling, and he was a co-captain as a freshman.

The Dantleys had heard tales of schools using neighbors to keep track of who came and left the homes at certain important prospects, but they dismissed them as the usual overblown talk—until Adrian visited North Carolina State on March 12.

An "avid fan, and friend of ours," managed to uncover not only the day of the visit but also the time and flight number, Dantley's mother says. During the visit someone phoned the N.C. State athletic department and asked if Dantley was there. When the secretary asked why the caller wanted to talk with Dantley, he hung up.

One airport, Raleigh-Durham, services Duke, North Carolina, and North Carolina State. Former Duke assistant Chuck Daly said the schools would hire bellhops, ticket agents, and others to keep tabs on who went where with whom. In fact, according to Daly, Duke was notified through its spy-like network that a player it coveted, Larry Miller, was going to North Carolina. Miller said the winner of the recruiting sweepstakes would be invited to his hometown in Pennsylvania for the signing ceremony, and, on Decision Eve, a travel agent called Duke with the news that Carolina coach Dean Smith was booked on the important flight.

Daly admitted spending six weeks of an eight-week period in Miller's hometown—"baby-sitting" it is called in the trade. In all, Duke is said to have spent $12,000 recruiting Miller, and it lost. Carolina landed Miller and advanced to the final four of the NCAA tournament in each of his final two varsity seasons, earning about $40,000 each time.

Most schools have their own flair. The highlight of some football prospects' visits to the University of Texas used to be a trip to the ranch of Longhorn booster Lyndon B. Johnson. Kansas recruits often can look forward to telegrams from Wilt Chamberlain, and of course a long chat with assistant athletic director Gale Sayers.

USC invited prized runners James McAlister and Kermit

Johnson (both of whom later went to UCLA) to sit on the bench with ex-Trojan O. J. Simpson at the 1970 Rose Bowl; Maryland coach Lefty Driesell placed an ad in the Washington *Post* with pictures of four area stars and the headline "We want you at the University of Maryland"; and UCLA, Houston, Maryland, Missouri, Kansas State, and Syracuse, among others, used coeds as campus guides and hostesses for prospects.

The University of Tennessee has published a lavish color brochure with photos of natives such as Elvis Presley, Davy Crockett, Andrew Jackson, and Estes Kefauver and a centerfold of a tanned, bikini-clad coed; and Maryland's basketball brochure, in the pre-Watergate days, had a cover of Tom McMillen and his parents meeting President and Mrs. Nixon at the White House.

When Peahead Walker was coaching football at Wake Forest, he would drive prospects through the nearby—and more prosperous-looking—Duke campus and pass it off as his own.

When John Thompson, now the Georgetown basketball coach, was being recruited two decades ago, Boston College thought he wanted to become a priest. They arranged an audience with Cardinal Cushing—and regretted it almost immediately. Thompson sat awe-struck for 45 minutes while the cardinal emphasized all the negative aspects of BC ("Son, they'll just treat you like a piece of meat") and the once-confident coaches shrank in their chairs. Thompson went to Providence.

"I just can't believe that a young man from New York would go to Hawaii or someone from Minnesota would go to Miami just for an education," says Jerry West of the Los Angeles Lakers, a native West Virginian who attended the state university and whose recruiting experiences were typical for most exceptionally gifted players. "I don't want to be specific but, yes, there were some offers you wouldn't believe. And this was right after the [betting/point-shaving] scandals and everyone supposedly was pretty cautious. Imagine what it would have been some other time."

Dantley heard the revealing we'll-take-care-of-you line from the peddlers. One said to come back with the best offer and his school would double it. When he was about to make a decision, the "bad-mouthing" by some coaches became especially frustrating.

"After Watergate, what do you expect these kids to think?" said the coach of an eastern university in his second year away from a school where no athletic scholarships were given. "My first year I kept coming in second, coming in second, coming in second and I didn't know what was going on. I had assistant coaches from other schools tell me I was never going to get the players. And it turned out it was true. I had a player this year ask me over the phone for money and I told him to go somewhere else if that's what he wanted. It turned out some 'friend of the university' told him we'd give him money. He didn't want to ask for it, but he was told to. He came to our place, and he's happy he did."

The Dantley and Buckley families both lived comfortably, and they emphasized that anyone offering more than the rules allow should knock on another door. Still, it was almost impossible to avoid the behind-their-backs whispers that frustrate every heavily recruited player.

When Adrian was a sophomore in high school, Mrs. Dantley, who worked for the Department of Agriculture, bought him a car—and a number of people insisted that it was his payment for playing at De Matha.

"I'm going to buy him another car in the fall," she said a month or so before her son selected his college, "and I know some people are going to claim Adrian got it from the college. Well, I don't care what they think. We do have to live a normal life."

Sometimes even the legal pitches leave a sour taste.

One Ivy League school told Buckley its scholarship was valued at $5,000 a year. However, the coach said, because that was based on living in the best dorm and eating in the best dining hall, Bruce might be able to pocket as much as $1,500 a year with a less handsome existence. Buckley said no, just as De Matha guard Bill Langloh declined a reported offer of some stereo equipment from a Southern Conference school.

Most prospects, parents, and coaches claim that recently imposed NCAA restrictions on entertainment and visits have been quite helpful. But the curbs also have created that seemingly contradictory tactic known as the under-the-table free meal.

"They claim they're taking them out on a 'friend' basis, not a prospect-coach basis," says coach Harry Rest of Washington's Mackin High, who had three excellent prospects—Larry Herron, David Reavis, and Larry Long—in 1973.

Letters and phone calls—at least one of each from the contending schools most weeks and more as the time for decision nears—remain the common tactic.

"It is a real pleasure to watch someone go at the game of basketball the way you do. . . . This is the kind of enthusiasm and dedication that I think was such an important part in the success of our team this past year. . . . I hope you are thinking about when you would like to visit Indiana as anytime would be fine with us. . . . I appreciate your taking the time to talk with me in Pittsburgh," read one special-delivery letter.

"We really believe that we can beat UCLA with the help

of Adrian Dantley. . . . It's great to be a Trojan," read one from Southern California.

"Adrian, in closing I want you to know I will dedicate myself to making your next four years the most successful and happiest you've ever experienced," read one especially passionate appeal from an assistant coach at a school Dantley nearly attended.

In most cases, the assistant coaches try to cement the sort of relationship that makes saying no as difficult as possible. They spend hours on the phone and days on the road. The most successful ones become head coaches. The unlucky— and Tom Weirich is one of the unluckiest—keep writing, phoning, and hoping.

Weirich was an assistant at Xavier University in Cincinnati and exceptionally close with Mackin's Herron, Reavis, and Long, who together were talented enough to cause a school to leap to national prominence. But when Xavier head coach Dick Campbell resigned, Weirich was not selected to replace him, instead becoming an assistant at Richmond.

"I have absolutely no doubt," says Mackin coach Rest, "that all three kids would have gone to Xavier had he become head coach."

The history of recruiting includes the West Virginia legislature declaring Rod Thorn a state asset to encourage him to attend the state university (he did) and the New Orleans city council passing a resolution asking 6-foot-10 citizen Rick Robey to attend Tulane (he went to Kentucky). No one, though, ever has endured what a Tulane assistant football coach named Tony Misita did to sign a lineman in January 1974.

But then Eric Lakso, 6-foot-6 and 281 pounds, was no ordinary prospect. He apparently was ready to sign a grant-in-aid until Misita arrived at Southbridge, Connecticut, with all the proper forms late one typically cold night. "I later found out it was five below zero, with a chill factor of minus thirty-five," Misita remembers. "Two high school coaching friends of mine met me at the airport and said Eric wanted to wait a week or two."

Misita was determined not to travel 2,000 miles for an unchallenged no, so he and the two high school coaches went to the Lakso home and were told by Eric that his father wanted to see them all in the family sauna outside.

Eric, the high school coaches, and Misita, all "buck naked," joined the father in the sauna, with Misita "biting a wet towel to try and stand the heat." In about 15 minutes, Misita saw the father whisper something to Eric. What he soon discovered was that the family was on a circulation kick—from extreme heat to extreme cold—and Eric was dispatched to chop a large hole in a nearby ice-covered pond.

Outside, the father quickly jumped into the pond, followed by Eric and the two high school assistants. The father suggested, rather strongly, that Misita also jump in. Misita, a southerner unaccustomed to snow let alone an experience such as this, balked momentarily. Then he considered losing Eric Lakso to Pitt or Boston College and immediately jumped into the freezing water.

"We go from there back into the sauna," Misita says, "and I'm just getting my senses back when we all go out for another trip to the pond." There was no hesitation on Misita's part the second time, since he had gone so far already, and when the five returned to the sauna the father said, "Coach, I'm going to let my boy go ahead and sign with Tulane."

Misita obviously had passed the test. He is convinced that Boston College could have signed Eric Lakso had their coaches just jumped a bit.

5 / The Coaches

LEFTY DRIESELL ONCE ADMITTED that recruiting was the one factor that could drive him to the professionals. Al McGuire, the Marquette basketball coach, has said the amount of money spent on the wooing of teen-age boys is "obnoxious, way out of line . . . pimpish." South Carolina's Frank McGuire calls recruiting "the toughest part of the whole thing. I don't think any of us like it." "When they get to the bottom of Watergate, they'll find a football coach," says Indiana's volatile Bobby Knight. "I think," says Notre Dame's Digger Phelps, "we've created a monster."

Even John Wooden, the man who annually fields the finest basketball team in the nation at UCLA, once insisted "I don't enjoy it, I never have." Wooden claims to have visited the homes of 12 to 15 players at the most in his 25 years of college coaching. Bill Walton's folks, of course, had the so-called Wizard of Westwood come knocking at their door.

So, too, did the parents of Kareem Abdul-Jabbar (then known as Lew Alcindor), in 1965. "But I visited Lewis only after he told me he would be coming to UCLA. His parents had met all the other coaches, and Lewis wanted them to meet me."

Once that was accomplished, any doubts the Alcindors may have harbored over the wisdom of sending their son 3,000 long miles away from New York City quickly vanished in the presence of this saintly soul.

One rival coach describes Wooden's charismatic technique as follows: "We thought we had a kid sewed up, but then Jesus Christ walked in. The kid's parents about fell over. How can you recruit against Jesus Christ?"

Quite obviously, not every coach makes that sort of an impression on an athlete or his parents. LSU basketball coach Dale Brown recalls recruiting one Mike Douglas, a rugged rebounder from Oakland, California, when he was an assistant at Utah State several seasons past.

"I recruited him for two years," Brown says. "Late in his senior year, I call him at home. 'I'd like to know what schools you've narrowed it down to,' I ask him. 'I just got one question to ask, coach,' he says to me. 'Have I visited Utah State yet?' "

UCLA, apparently, has no such identity problems. People tend to remember audiences with John Wooden.

"Our success has made it a bit easier," Wooden modestly proclaims. "But personally, it's very difficult, one of the least desirable things we have to do."

Wooden has never done very much recruiting himself. He prefers that his assistants, Frank Arnold and Gary Cunningham, do most of the legwork. "I'll handle the coaching," says the man whose teams have set an all-time NCAA record with 88 straight victories.

"Most of my personal contact is on the campus. We like

to have the parents visit whenever possible. And I enjoy talking to them when they come. But visiting the home, I'm a little against that. That's applying a little more pressure than I really care for."

Most of the pressure, then, is applied by his assistants. First it was Jerry Norman, who recruited Gail Goodrich, Walt Hazzard, and Alcindor, among others, before resigning abruptly after the 1968 season to become a stockbroker. Norman was followed by Denny Crum, who rounded up most of the Walton Gang to Westwood before leaving to accept the head post at Louisville in 1971. Now Arnold, a former Oregon assistant who joined the UCLA staff shortly after Crum left it, handles the awesome responsibility of supplying the players for the most successful team in the history of college basketball.

Wooden demands that his assistants concentrate as much as possible on the southern California area for talent and says, with considerable pride, "90 per cent of our lettermen are from the state." Wooden also insists UCLA simply will not recruit an out-of-state prospect unless the youngster makes the first move. Alcindor's high school coach, Jack Donahue, for example, wrote Wooden about America's most highly sought-after prep player.

If Donahue had not contacted the school about Alcindor, would UCLA have let it go at that?

"We'll never know, will we?" Wooden says with an impish chuckle.

Larry Farmer, a starting forward on the Bruins' 1972 championship team, sent the coach a clipping from a Denver newspaper detailing a particularly impressive performance in a game during his senior year.

Adrian Dantley, who had been contacted by almost every school known to mankind, was not actively recruited by UCLA "because he never told us he was interested,"

Arnold explained. "I've got his name sitting in front of me now," Arnold said in May 1973, less than a month before Dantley finally settled on Notre Dame as the school in his future. "If he wrote now, I don't know what we'd do."

As it turned out, the Bruins did not regret their decision not to go after Dantley. They turned up a fellow by the name of Marques Johnson, a powerfully built forward from Los Angeles who cracked the starting lineup in midseason and made a major contribution in the Bruins' ascent to the Final Four in Greensboro.

Dantley says he was not particularly interested in heading west because Wooden, then 62 and plagued by a minor heart ailment, was publicly contemplating retirement. Dantley felt that he probably would not have been around to coach him the full four years.

Wooden says he is constantly amazed to read in the newspaper of a youngster signing at another school, then telling the world he had narrowed his choices down to three, one of them UCLA. "I've seen it happen quite frequently, and I've never even heard of the youngster," Wooden says. "In no way, shape, or form did we recruit that boy. But there it is, plain as day: 'UCLA was among his choices.' "

Unlike most schools which recruit en masse, hoping that two or three of the ten players actively wooed may eventually sign and make it to the varsity someday, Wooden and his staff have been extremely selective over the years. In 1974 UCLA went after five prospects and landed all of them, according to Arnold. The previous three years they were five-for-five, two-for-three, and three-for-three.

Arnold, Cunningham, and occasionally Wooden scour the summer leagues of southern California for talent, then narrow the list down to a dozen players they consider potential UCLA starters.

"In the fall," Wooden says, "the first thing we do is to get his transcript. If he qualifies, we obviously want to determine his basketball abilities. We talk to coaches of teams he played against, and his own coach. His citizenship and character also are very important to us."

The staff then determines the number of players they actually will need—"I don't recruit in numbers," Wooden repeats, often—and informs the prospects the school covets that they will be recruited.

"I don't like this idea of selling a youngster," Wooden says. "I don't like a pushy recruiter. I want the player to come to us. If we don't have a program good enough to sell, they shouldn't come. If they have doubts in their minds, they should go somewhere where there is no doubt. I want to be sure a youngster wants us. That's important."

Arnold or Cunningham usually makes the initial contact with a prospect in the fall. "We tell a youngster 'We're interested in you, but we won't bother you,'" says Arnold. "We sit back, we keep very casual, occasional contact, just to let them know we're around. We won't pound, pound, pound. We think sometimes they get obligated to a particular school, and are almost afraid to say no."

Precisely that sort of dilemma confronted Gavin Smith, a 6-foot-6 forward from Sherman Oaks, California, described by many recruiters as "the best white prospect in America" in 1973.

By early spring of his senior year at Van Nuys High School, Smith had narrowed his choices to Hawaii, Washington State, and UCLA. Then it became State and its coach, George Raveling, a man he deeply admired, or UCLA and Wooden, a man he worshipped.

"I really want to help George," Smith said in his hotel room that April after the Dapper Dan tournament. "He's just the greatest. He had a lot to do with me being in this game and starting. We're very close. He writes letters my mom actually cries over they're so good.

"But I truly know UCLA is best for me, no matter what everyone says, and I'm just going to have to come out and tell that to George. It'll be hard.

"I've sat with Wooden before [UCLA] games and sometimes I forget who he is. Then I look around and all those people are looking at him and it hits me—here I am with John Wooden. It's the ultimate mind-blower."

Smith said Wooden told him only three prospects had the potential to start for him as freshmen: Lew Alcindor, Bill Walton, and Gavin Smith. "Well," said Smith, "I'd like to get on a PA system to the world and shout 'Wooden told me I had a chance to start as a freshman.' And he won't buy me a sandwich, because it will be termed my one meal the rules allow and he said he wants to have it with my parents."

A few days after the Dapper Dan, Smith made his decision—UCLA—and phoned the Hawaii coach, Bruce O'Neil, to give him the news. O'Neil was cordial, told him he would have been better off at Hawaii, but wished him good fortune nevertheless.

Then Smith made the call he had dreaded, to Raveling, only to find that the head coach was in the Midwest on a recruiting trip. Smith informed State assistant coach John Heft of his decision, and asked him to have Raveling call. Smith wanted to tell Raveling why himself, man-to-man.

Two months later, Raveling had not returned the call. "I thought we could at least talk about it," Smith says. "The whole family's disappointed because we got to know each other so well. And he won't even give us a call."

Raveling also had hired Smith's high school coach, Bert Golden, for his summer camp. Two days after Smith had signed with UCLA, a letter arrived informing Golden the position was unavailable. "That's the way it goes in the recruiting world," says Smith with a shrug.

While Smith no doubt would have been a starter at Washington State, or anywhere else, he languished on the UCLA bench his freshman season, in 1974, even playing occasionally with the junior varsity team. "I don't regret the decision one bit," Smith insisted during the 1974 NCAA tournament at Greensboro. "I love the school, and I'm going to play here. I'm not worried about it at all. Would I be here [at the tournament] if I had gone to State or anywhere else? I'm satisfied, very satisfied."

Before he signed on, Wooden urged Smith, as he urges every one of his school's prospects, to meet his players, all of them, even the disgruntled substitute that inevitably crops up every year. "They can find out more from the players than anyone else," Wooden says. "I especially want them to talk to the players who play the same position. A youngster may not like the way we do certain things, and that gives him the opportunity to find out before it's too late."

UCLA usually offers the scholarship after the high school basketball season has ended. "We don't want to put any more pressure on a youngster than necessary," Arnold says. "It's not our way." Nor, apparently, is it the UCLA way to moan when a player decides he would be happier elsewhere. Many of his colleagues, Wooden complains, "automatically cry foul when another school gets a youngster they are after."

One Far West coach cried foul against UCLA for its recruiting of Sidney Wicks, who went on to become a No. 1 draft choice in the National Basketball Association.

"There was no way UCLA could get him in as a freshman," says the coach, a head man now and an assistant when Wicks was in high school in 1968. "We could get him into our place, and I really thought Sidney was interested. In fact, he told me he wanted to come. So I went back to LA to sign him. I get to his house—and nobody's there. I don't mean no one was home, I mean that apartment was empty: furniture, TV sets, everything. I looked everywhere for him and I finally found one of his friends on the playground. 'Oh, yeah,' he says, 'Sidney moved to Santa Monica. I don't know where.'

"I tried for a couple of days to find him in Santa Monica, but no one knew where he was. Finally, I just gave up. I've got some pride, too. Then he enrolls in junior college, and two years later he's playing for UCLA. I saw him once since then and I asked him, 'What happened, Sidney?' 'Aw,' he says, 'you know how those things are, coach. Hope there's no hard feelings.'

"I respect John Wooden so much as a person and as a man and as a coach, and I just hope and pray that the dynasty wasn't built on cheating. I don't believe it was, and if it was, I believe Wooden didn't know anything about it. But that Sidney Wicks story keeps flashing through my mind, and it makes you wonder."

Wooden heard all of the talk, the whispered innuendoes, and he still insists that "I deeply feel most of the things you hear about cheating are in the minds of the people who miss out. I haven't ever felt there is as much going on as most people think. Coaches are too suspicious of each other. Most of what you hear is suspicion, not fact."

"Bad publicity makes things appear worse than they really are," says John McKay, the Southern Cal football coach. "Too many people make statements that have no basis in fact. What creates a lot of animosity is that three-fourths of the stuff you hear is untrue."

But many other coaches strongly disagree.

"I don't think you can win big without cheating," says Pepperdine College basketball coach Gary Colson.

"This is the worst year I've ever seen for cheating," said Ed Murphy when he resigned in 1974 as New Mexico State's chief basketball recruiter.

Says Texas football coach Darrell Royal: "You're out there trying to sell yourself and your school and the prospect ain't hearing a word you're saying. All he's wondering is when you're going to start talking money."

But Wooden, ever the saintly optimist, will hear none of it. "I have always lived on the principle that if you trust, you will be disappointed occasionally," he says. "But if you mistrust, you'll be miserable all the time."

John Wooden probably is not the only college coach in America who insists he puts serious stock in a prospect's citizenship and character. But he is the only man ever to coach seven straight national championships. No one is likely to approach that remarkable feat, nor the 88 straight victories, nor the string of 38 straight triumphs in NCAA championship competition snapped in the 1974 semifinals by the eventual national champions, North Carolina State.

But the rest certainly can try, and, as South Carolina's Frank McGuire has said, "X's and O's are fine, but you gotta have the players to execute 'em." And that is why the mad scramble continues.

Every blue-chip prospect in the fold means a step closer to sold-out arenas, national attention, television gold, and, best of all for the coaches, security. There is money, big money, to be made coaching a college basketball team. Dale Brown, the LSU head coach, was offered the head job at Oral Roberts University in 1974. Oral himself jetted in at least twice to fly Brown back to his Tulsa campus. He offered him $35,000 a year in salary, a $60,000 home Brown could eventually sell and pocket the proceeds from, and a 2,000-bed summer camp (one of the big coaching money-makers), as well as an unlimited recruiting budget and a staff of three full-time assistants. But Brown was not all that interested. "Oral told me it was God's will that Dale Brown be the next head coach at Oral Roberts University," Brown says. "I told him I had thought about it for a long time and I had prayed to God myself. I said that God told me to stay at LSU. What could he say?"

Coaching can be a lonely job, as well—particularly for the assistants—of one-night stands in drab motels, rushed meals at the nearest available coffee shop, and midnight flights to Boondock, U.S.A., not to mention countless appearances before glad-handing alumni groups, booster clubs, and, of course, parents of potential prospects. Wives, mistresses, girl friends, and children are usually left behind, occasionally for weeks at a time. Life merely becomes a succession of bouncing basketballs.

In 1955, Dick Schafrath was an all-state fullback in Wooster, Ohio, a big ol' strapping farm boy who had America's college coaches—particularly Woody Hayes of Ohio State and Kentucky's Blanton Collier—lining up at the front door for an audience.

Most coaches left after the perfunctory living room spiel, but a Kentucky assistant went one better. It was spring planting time and there were all sorts of chores to be done around the Schafrath spread. So he merely pitched in.

"Yeah, he'd come by and stay a couple or three nights on the farm," Schafrath recalled recently. "He helped my dad build a barn, did some work out in the fields—that kind of thing. I was usually around, too, and we'd talk football and all that. Nah, he didn't get paid anything, but he had three good meals a day. My mother saw to that."

But Mrs. Schafrath also was partial to Ohio State. Woody Hayes told her that young Dick owed it to the people in his state to come to Columbus, and she agreed.

Every time Schafrath called the people at Kentucky for a chat, he said, his mother would place a call to Hayes and make him get on the line.

The Kentucky assistant wound up working on the farm for about three weeks. He lived in an upstairs bedroom and also managed to take off a few pounds in the field, as well, so it was not a total loss when young Dick Schafrath signed to go to Ohio State.

The assistant coach left the farm shortly after that, and went on to bigger and better things. His name was Bill Arnsparger, and today he is the head coach of the New York Giants.

For Schafrath, and most of the other Buckeye players, life was free and fairly easy at Ohio State. They allegedly were to be holding down jobs that would defray the cost of their tuition and provide them with a little extra spending money. "The big joke around town was that my job was to turn the lights off at the stadium," Schafrath said. "Of course, there weren't any lights. There still aren't."

"All we used to do was show up at the stadium and study for a couple of hours, and that was the job. You didn't do anything."

Dale Brown took a $3,600 pay cut when he left a high school job in Palm Springs, California, to become an assistant at Utah State. "I worked like a dog," he recalls. "If I didn't, they'd find somebody else who could."

Maryland's Lefty Driesell simply thrives on hard work. He has been known to push himself, and his staff, 14 to 16 hours a day, seven days a week, pursuing America's most talented players.

Moses Malone and a flock of the nation's top schoolboy

stars came to Washington, D.C., in March 1974 to participate in an all-star game at the Capital Centre. The day of the game Driesell just happened to be the only coach at the table when the young heroes were treated to lunch in the Senate dining room.

After the game the players and several dozen college coaches headed back to a motel in nearby Lanham, Maryland, to drink a little beer, eat some cheeseburgers sent over by the sponsoring restaurant chain, and swap stories. The hospitality suite was located on the tenth floor of the Sheraton Lanham Hotel. Driesell rented a room down the hall, and prospects shuffled in and out all night listening to his pitch. His entire staff and a half-dozen of his players were in the hotel. The players escorted several of the young giants to a private party when the hospitality room ceased being hospitable.

"I don't care if he eats green cheese and barks at the moon," Maryland athletic director Jim Kehoe once said, "as long as he wins games and puts fans in the stands."

Sitting in his office one day after the 1973 season, Driesell talked about his high-pressure approach. "How I recruit depends on what I need," he said. "I recruit on defense and attitude as much as I do speed. I also like to have a shot blocker. But mostly it's hard work. My assistant coaches do a great deal of it. You have to have a good product to sell. And we do.

"One thing I insist on. I don't like to say anything derogatory about another school or another coach. If other coaches do, they won't last long. People don't want.to hear it."

At that point, the outer office phone rang and Joe Harrington, an assistant coach, broke in to tell Driesell a prospect was on the line.

"Oh, oh," the coach said, and a few seconds later his

worst fears had been confirmed. A midwestern prospect had called to say he would be attending Kansas, not Maryland, the following fall.

Driesell was not smiling, though he remained cordial as the painful conversation continued. "Well, Roger, I'm sorry to lose you, but I respect your decision," he said, finally. "If you're in the area this summer, don't hesitate to come on over and use our court. We'd love to have you. Good-bye."

Certainly it was not the first time Driesell had lost an outstanding player. At Davidson, he had signed Charlie Scott to a Southern Conference letter of intent only to have the future All-America eventually wind up at North Carolina. Driesell does not like to talk about that case, nor of the alleged bad feeling it provoked toward North Carolina coach Dean Smith at the time. "I have all the respect in the world for Coach Smith," Driesell said. "Let's leave it at that."

This sort of intense recruiting rivalry is not uncommon, however. "Actually, coaches don't get angry with each other over coaching," says Georgia Tech football coach Pepper Rodgers. "Basically, we're all friends. But we do get angry over *players,* over who's playing for whom and how this player got to that school. And that's something caused 99 per cent of the time by one thing—recruiting."

Occasionally the hassles have become physical. In 1965 Tommy Prothro, then the head football coach at UCLA, went to Hershey, Pennsylvania, to speak with Jerry Levias, a gifted wide receiver from Beaumont, Texas, and a teammate. Southern Methodist, the school Levias finally attended, heard that UCLA was after their Main Man, so they sent an assistant coach, Chuck Curtis, to Hershey. The two clashed outside the locker room after the game.

"Curtis grabbed me and started hollering," Prothro told Jeff Prugh of the Los Angeles *Times.* "I told him I'd been 24 years in college coaching and never saw anything like it, that I certainly didn't intend to get into a brawl with him in front of ladies and these kids and I didn't like some of the language he used."

Curtis had another version. "Suddenly, here came Prothro blocking our path. He asked the boys if they would like to fly back to California with him, and I told Prothro they were already signed and sealed for SMU and I was going to see that they were delivered. . . . Prothro got angry and a little obnoxious and would not let us by him. All I did was shove him against a fence and see to it that he didn't bother the boys."

"It's like there are two seasons—the basketball season and the recruiting season," says Georgetown coach John Thompson. "For some of these people, it doesn't really matter which championship you win."

It has been that way in the Atlantic Coast Conference ever since the late Everett Case left Indiana and moseyed on down Tobacco Road to North Carolina State in 1946. He brought a fistful of players with him that year, and his first team, known as the "Hoosier Hotshots," finished 26-5, the best record in the school's history until the Wolfpack went undefeated in 1972–73.

Case, who once told a friend "You can buy a hell of a player for $35 a month," is generally credited with upgrading the ACC to the point where many now consider it the finest basketball conference in America. The other schools simply had to compete with him for talent, or else be content to play for No. 2.

South Carolina's Frank McGuire followed in Case's footsteps at North Carolina in the 1950s, importing then as he does now most of his material from the New York metropolitan area. Vic Bubas, a former Case assistant, was

considered the wiliest—and most successful—ACC recruiter during the 1960s. Now everyone is involved.

According to informed sources, the average ACC basketball recruiting budget is $35,000, with Clemson—a team
now on the verge of winning big—the most lavish spender
at $70,000 a year. But recruiting costs are rather easy to
disguise in other budget categories.

The Pacific Eight Conference averages closer to $15,000 a
year, with UCLA a few thousand below that figure and
Washington State, the highest, a few thousand above. In
1972 the Pullman, Washington, school hired one of the
most energetic, and knowledgeable, basketball recruiters in
America, former Maryland assistant George Raveling, the
only black head coach in the conference. As an assistant at
Villanova, he recruited All-America Howard Porter to that
school. Most of Maryland's black upperclassmen are there
because of Raveling. His major responsibility at the school
was recruiting.

There are some who maintain that pressure on the
assistant is the prime catalyst for cheating. If an assistant
lands the better players, the program will flourish, and so
will the job opportunities for him as a head coach somewhere else.

"But if you lose," says Raveling, "they'll fire your boss
and you'll go too. The most pressure when I was an
assistant was self-imposed. I never felt the pressure of being
fired. I was cocky enough to think that I could get another
job anywhere in the country, so why worry?"

"Assistant coaches," says Louisville's Crum, "have no
security, no tenure, and usually a one-year contract. It's a
very nebulous position at best. You get none of the credit
for winning, and all the blame because you didn't recruit
the right people. Everyone knows you can't win without the

kids, and whose fault is it if you don't get them? There is just a tremendous amount of pressure, and that's why some people take shortcuts."

A 1972 survey by the Fellowship of Christian Athletes polled 107 coaches. Thirty said most coaches skirt the rules in recruiting. A majority said the rules are possible to abide by, but some others said "it's impossible to recruit honestly."

"You've got to cheat in recruiting to win," says Bob Cousy, former head coach at Boston College. "Competition is fierce. If a school becomes too flagrant and is charged with irregularities, there's a lot of buck passing. Usually, though, it's the coach who winds up getting fired."

Raveling insists he does not cheat. Like Driesell, he believes in exhausting work. But Mike Young, who went to Manhattan, had another story.

"Me and four other dudes they were recruiting were flown out there [to Washington State]," Young told Dick Klayman of the New York *Post* in December 1973, "and when we got off the plane there was Coach Raveling and three of his assistants. The first one would say 'How do you do' and pass you right on to the next one. It was a receiving line right there at the airport.

"Then they handed us this schedule telling us what we would do and when we would be doing it for the whole weekend. One of the events was a meeting with Coach Raveling.

"He said, 'We have alumni who can take care of you. They don't give you any money but if you want to go home for a weekend or anything like that. . . .'

"You knew just what he was talking about, even if it was in an indirect way. But I really liked the cat, his personality overshadowed everything."

Raveling has since denied the allegation, and also said, "I

get sick hearing 'Well, I lost him to Washington State because they gave him this and that.' You outhustle them, and then they say you bought 'em. It's not true, a lot of guys use that as an escape. A lot of guys are standing around boozing at the hotel bar, or chasing babes, when they should be working."

While Wooden prefers to keep the pressure off a recruit as much as possible, Raveling starts hammering away from the first moment the rules allow—the first day of school— until a prospect finally makes up his mind.

"I try to keep my calls down to something realistic. I try to find out if the parents encourage a lot of contact," he says. "I do a lot of correspondence. I'd say 50 per cent of my recruiting is done by mail. We usually try to write to our top prospects once a week. I want it to be something personal, something of substance."

Raveling's entire recruiting philosophy is based on the premise that "the better a kid knows me, the more rapport I've got with a kid, the more confidence he's going to have in me and the harder it is for him to tell me no."

Occasionally, though, there are hard feelings, as with Gavin Smith. Raveling, when interviewed in the spring of 1973, had also recently informed a player, one of several forwards he was recruiting, that he could not offer a scholarship simply because the youngster had waited too long to make his decision.

"I had to sign the other people because we couldn't take a chance on him changing his mind," Raveling said. "His parents are very upset, but sometimes you have to operate on a first-come, first-serve basis. But the kid has a certain responsibility too. All the time you spend on him, and then he drops you. It works both ways. We screw up too, I'll admit that. His folks are pissed off at me. But I can sleep at night."

Al McGuire, the Marquette coach, has never deemed it necessary—or practical—to get all that involved. He simply cannot afford to. Marquette budgets a million dollars for its seven sports, compared to the $4 million at Ohio State or $3 million at Harvard, and his recruiting budget is less than $10,000 a year.

"I move in for the final hit," says McGuire, a slick New York hustler who is among the most outspoken and brutally honest of all his coaching colleagues. "I'm a late recruiter. I scare the dickens out of a school, I scare 'em to death. What I like is for a kid to get it down to two or three schools. Let 'em eliminate each other, then move in when it really counts."

McGuire's formula worked to perfection with Butch Lee, the No. 1 guard prospect in America last year. Lee, from DeWitt Clinton in the Bronx, had narrowed his choices to Duke and Penn before Marquette entered the picture in February. He signed to play with the Warriors in April.

"I get tired talking about the dental school, the second best math department," says McGuire. "I just try and tell the kids this is the second greatest decision you're going to make in your life. The first is who you marry, and that's not something you do by turning on the sunshine and looking at the water fountains.

"It's a tough decision, and a kid better know exactly what he's looking for, or he'll get taken for a ride, believe me."

While Al McGuire lets his assistants, particularly Hank Raymond, handle a good share of the paper- and legwork, Frank McGuire at South Carolina oversees his highly successful recruiting program himself. He also starts after prospects earlier than most. McGuire first spotted Brian Winters, his All-America guard, in 1974, at a summer camp in the Catskills when he was 14 years old. He offered Bill Bradley a scholarship his sophomore year in high school.

"I got a letter from a very good and trusted friend about Bradley," McGuire says. "So I went out to see the kid play in Missouri and I offered him a scholarship on the spot. His father thought I was crazy. But I was right, oh was I right."

Frank McGuire is considered by many of his peers as the most proficient recruiter of them all. Dick Grubar, an assistant coach at Florida who played at North Carolina, recalls that his own coach in high school had said "unless I wanted to go to South Carolina, don't talk to Coach McGuire." Grubar never did, until he had enrolled at Chapel Hill.

"I study a prospect as much as they study me," McGuire says. "We scout them all the time. We watch their high school games and we watch the playgrounds. I have a lot of contacts in New York City, and they help, too.

"A big selling point with me is that I've played pro basketball, I've coached pro basketball, and I know the pro game thoroughly. If a boy shows any potential at all in that direction, I'll point him the right way.

"I'll tell you, recruiting used to be a hell of a lot of fun. Sometimes, it gets too damned complicated now."

6 / A Recruiting Trip

On April 22, 1974, Dale Brown, head basketball coach at Louisiana State University, boarded a jet in Baton Rouge and headed north. He was on a business trip, one that would last three days and take him to Manhattan, Brooklyn, Queens, and the Bronx, to Baltimore and finally Washington, D.C. His business? Recruiting basketball players.

In Brown's second year as the school's head coach, his team had won only 12 of its 26 games and finished eighth in the Southeastern Conference, a 10-team league. Plainly, he needed help.

The forty-one-year-old Brown is not your ordinary basketball coach. Betrayed only by a slightly receding forehead, he is an imposing figure of a man, always impeccably attired in stylish suits and patent-leather shoes. He was born and raised in Minot, North Dakota, and was a 12-letter star at Minot State Teachers' College. He put in his time as a coach on the junior and senior high school level in South Dakota and California for eight years, then moved on in 1966 to an assistant's job at Utah State. When coach Ladell Anderson quit to join the professionals in 1971, Brown assumed he would get the head job. Instead, "he got screwed," according to Marvin Roberts, one of his former players. "He's the only man who should have been given that job. The players loved the man, all of us, black and white. He was a great coach."

Stung by his snub at Utah State, Brown spent a year as an assistant at Washington State before LSU beckoned in 1972 to rebuild its sagging basketball fortunes. In his first season, he took a team picked by Southeastern Conference writers to win two games all year and pushed them to a 14-12 record. They called that outfit "the Hustlers," simply because they dove for every loose ball, scrapped for every rebound, and played the tightest defense ever seen in those parts.

That same year, Brown was out pushing basketball in the state, drumming up support for his team and his program. With money out of his own pocket, he purchased 1,000 basketball nets, packed them in the trunk of his car, and started touring the state, from the bayous to the big cities. Every time he saw a backyard basket, he stopped the car, knocked on the door, introduced himself, and handed out a free net. He sent chalk holders to every high school coach in the state, then peppered them with pocket change-purses, key-chains, and inspirational poems and messages from the basketball staff.

He spoke at dinners, luncheons, Chamber of Commerce meetings. He recruited former LSU stars Bob Pettit, Dr. Billy Cannon, and Pete Maravich to talk with prospects. Within two years he had moved LSU's program into the twentieth century.

Now Brown was jetting to New York City, looking for players to help his program. And this particular trip was a little different than most. Brown had agreed to take along a reporter as he delivered his pitch to some of America's most highly sought-after players.

"I don't want to deceive anyone, tell them you're my assistant coach or anything like that," he said. "I'll introduce you as my friend. I want you to see recruiting as it really is."

When he arrived in New York that chilly April day, Brown had already signed three players for his program, though none was of the blue-chip, high school All-America variety. He was looking now for a penetrating guard, one who could set up his offense, score in double figures, and play defense, and a rugged rebounding forward to replace the graduating Collis Temple, who had averaged 15 points and 10 rebounds a game.

From Kennedy Airport in Queens, Brown took a taxi downtown, to the midtown Manhattan law offices of Lew Schaffel. Brown and Schaffel had met several years before while the attorney was representing Marvin Roberts in his professional negotiations. A graduate of Howard University's law school, Schaffel also represented professional basketball players Austin Carr, Earl Monroe, and Tiny Archibald.

Schaffel made a comfortable living, drove a late-model Porsche, and had recently purchased a home in an exclusive Connecticut suburb. He was also a 30-year-old basketball freak, a Brooklyn boy who still thrilled at the prospect of going one-on-one at the neighborhood courts.

Often after a long day in the office, he would change to shorts and sneakers and head out to the playgrounds around the city to play a little ball. Though affluent, longhaired, white, and Jewish, he was accepted by black athletes. For the last few years, Schaffel and his partner, Jerry Davis, had hired a number of young black high school kids to work part-time in their office, running errands, going for coffee, delivering messages across town.

One of those kids was Al Green, who had worked in Schaffel's office in the summer of 1972. Dale Brown wanted Green for his program, and Schaffel set up a meeting in his office as soon as Brown arrived from the airport.

Green, a 6-1 guard, had recently completed a season at the Maine Central Institute, a private school in Pittsfield. He had attended Harlem Prep in Manhattan the year before, but in the summer of his senior season he was told the school would be closing because of lack of funds. He was 19 years old at the time, too old to play in the public school league.

In his playground wanderings, Green had run into Rodney Parker, who had two passions in life. For a living, he allegedly hawked tickets at Madison Square Garden. For satisfaction, he placed basketball players in college.

Parker had sent Jim McMillian to Columbia—"Go where you'll make the program," he told him—and had recently rescued James (Fly) Williams from the streets of Brooklyn by helping him get into a private prep school in upstate New York and then convincing tiny Austin Peay State College in Tennessee to take a chance on giving Williams a scholarship. Two years later, The Fly had broken every Austin Peay scoring record and had been offered $1 million to sign with the Denver Rockets.

Parker also was one of Schaffel's close friends—"Sooner or later, anyone who plays ball in this city runs into Rodney," Schaffel said—and together they helped get Green into Maine Central. In his senior year Green averaged 39 points, 11 rebounds, and 7 assists a game, scored a state record of 56 points in one affair, and led his team to its conference championship.

Green was named high school All-America, and a month after the season ended he was invited to play in the prestigious Dapper Dan all-star game. Brown was there, too, and introduced himself at one of the practices. They chatted briefly, and Brown promised to look up Green in New York.

And so they met on the afternoon of April 22 in a back room in Schaffel's office. The discussion lasted no more than an hour. It was friendly, low key, and mostly one-sided. Brown did most of the talking. "I saw right away that I could trust coach Brown," Green recalled a few months after the meeting. "Lewie told me all aoout him, and I was really impressed. He was straight, I could see that. I dug the man, we hit it off. No pressure, nothing like that. He told me about his school, about his program, and I told him it sounded great, but I wasn't interested unless I could be sure I'd get the ball some. But he didn't promise me anything. I liked that."

The recruiters had begun knocking on Green's door during his junior year at Harlem Prep, and his last season in Maine had been extremely hectic. The phone never stopped ringing, he said, and each day's mail brought another batch of recruiting letters. Two days before he met with Brown, he had returned from his fifteenth recruiting trip. He had been to Texas–El Paso, Maryland, Dayton, Iowa, Florida State, and Hawaii, among others. And he had received his share of illegal offers.

One coach, Green said almost matter-of-factly, offered a car, another said he would move his mother into a new house. But Al Green apparently was not interested. For one, he had been warned by a man from the NCAA about accepting anything other than a scholarship, room, board, and laundry money. And for another, he had principles of his own. "If they buy you and you don't produce," he said, "it's like they own you. I don't want anybody owning me.

"In the beginning it was nice, but after a while, you start hearing the same lines, and they all start to sound the same. At one school, an alumnus offered me $5,000 if I'd sign. It really turned me off. I'll get it in the future. I don't need it now."

When the April 22 meeting in Schaffel's office was over, Brown drove Green home to the Bronx. He lived in a quiet neighborhood, a few blocks off the Grand Concourse. Al introduced his mother to the coach.

"Don't mind the way the place looks," she said. "We just moved in a couple of weeks ago. It's a mess. Oh, the other place was terrible, but we only paid $73 a month. This here place cost $172. And now, the elevator don't even work." Inside, the furniture was faded and the bare wooden floors were badly warped. But they also were immaculate, and freshly waxed. Al's trophies were piled on a table in the living room.

Mrs. Green obviously was not prepared for company. A short, rotund woman with huge arms and a radiant grin, she seemed slightly flustered by the tall white man in the neatly pressed suit sitting now on her lumpy beige couch. "Where did you say you were from?" she asked several times as Brown talked to her about Louisiana State. Brown told her about himself, how poor he had been as a child, that he had never slept on a bed until he was 21 years old. He told her about the one-room apartment he shared alone with his mother after his father had abandoned them when he was only three days old.

He told her about Baton Rouge, about the city's large black population, the 2,500 black students on campus, the black student body president.

"You're very fortunate, Mrs. Green," he said. "You have a wonderful son, and he's going to make you very proud some day. You know, a few years back, I sat in the living room of Mr. and Mrs. Roberts over in Brooklyn and I told them that some day their son would make them proud. You know what? He signed a pro contract for $500,000 a few years ago, and the first thing he did was move his mother and father out of the projects."

"Oh, that's nice," Mrs. Green said.

Al stayed out of the living room during the entire discussion. Only when it was time for Brown to leave did he return. As they walked out into the hallway, Mrs. Green asked again, "Where did you say you were from?"

"Louisiana State, in Baton Rouge," Brown said patiently.

"That anywhere near Morgan City?" she asked.

"Why sure, that's just a couple of miles away," he answered.

"You know, Al's grandparents live in Morgan City," she said.

Brown's eyes popped wide open. "You're kidding, what are their names? Al, you didn't tell me that."

"Yeah, coach, I guess I forgot. I never even thought about it."

"Well, what are their names, Mrs. Green?"

"Mr. and Mrs. Frank Verrett," she said.

"Well, listen, as soon as I get back down there, I'm going to go look them up and say hello. Geez, Al, imagine that. Your grandparents down there, that's unbelievable."

Mrs. Green smiled broadly, and invited Brown back. "You come back and we'll have some chicken legs and cake next time. I want you to come back now, you hear?"

Al accompanied Brown down the six flights of stairs to Brown's car, borrowed from a friend of Schaffel's. "I'll call you back and we'll set up that visit, Big Al," Brown said.

With that, Brown ducked into the car and was off, heading back to Schaffel's office downtown with the reporter.

"Do you see what I mean about schools prostituting these kids?" he said, trying to compete with Third Avenue traffic. "What's Al Green supposed to think of a guy who offered him $5,000 to play for him, what's he supposed to think about that guy who offered his mother a house? Hey, these are proud people. She said they paid $172 a month for that apartment. Did you see how clean it was? Not a speck of dust. That tells me something about Al, too. He's a proud kid. Sure he has trouble with directions, probably has trouble reading, too. But that's no problem. We can get him in, and when we get him in we'll put him through these tests. We'll have tutors for him in every course. We'll find out what he's deficient in, and we'll get someone to work with him.

"Imagine that, though, his grandparents living right there in Morgan City, Louisiana. That's unbelievable. I don't know if we're gonna get Al Green, but I think he trusts me. We'll go right down to the wire with him, I know that."

A few blocks from Schaffel's office, Brown suddenly whipped the car into a narrow U-turn. He had spotted a familiar face. "Rodney, Rodney Parker!" he yelled out the window. "Hey, it's me, Dale."

Parker waved hello; Brown parked the car and greeted his old friend with a warm handshake. Parker is 37 and looks 10 years younger. He was wearing jeans and a flowered shirt, open at the neck. His Afro was high, wide, and handsome, and his smile quick and easy.

"Hey, coach, I got a super for you," Parker said as they walked down the street. "Bernard King, everybody wants him, 6-5, big strong kid. Went to Fort Hamilton in Brooklyn. All-city. Goes to the hoop like you can't believe.

And he's got a little brother, Al. He's 14. Coach, he's better right now than David Thompson was when he was a senior in high school. No shit. You interested?"

" 'Course I'm interested," Brown said.

"I think he's playing tomorrow night, they got a game out at Pace College, New York kids against some Russian youth team. Everybody'll be there." Brown said he would be, too.

Back in Schaffel's office, Brown went to check in with his staff at LSU; Parker flopped into a chair in an adjacent room.

Rodney's most celebrated reclamation case was Fly Williams. "Hey, he was a bad dude, a really bad dude," Parker said, shaking his head. "The summer before he's supposed to go to college, he punches a ref in the stomach in a summer game. Who wants a kid like that? Nobody. That's when I step in.

"The coaches will find their way to the good high school players, but there are so many kids they miss, it's unreal. I go after the kids nobody else wants. I don't get nothing out of it but satisfaction. I don't need the money.

"But these kids got nobody, nobody at all. Most of 'em wind up in the streets anyway. But I helped a lot of 'em.

"Some of these kids are so naive. They don't realize that they're not as great as they think they are. They all think they can go to a school and be All-America.

"You know what I tell my kids? Go where you'll be the king, man, the mother-fucking king. You think Fly would be All-America if he didn't get his 30 shots a game? I sent him to Austin Peay. Whoever heard of Austin Peay before Fly Williams got there? Now you know that once he's there, they're not recruiting anybody better than he is. Maybe after he leaves and the program is more established. But for four years, he is The Man, the Main Man, you dig?

"So many of these kids go to the big schools, and they get lost in the shuffle. They get grade trouble, they get ineligible, and all of a sudden you never hear from them again. I know where my kids go, they'll be the whole ball game, the king, man, the king. That's what it's all about."

Brown, by this time, had completed his business.

"Bernard King, man, Bernard King," Parker kept repeating. "This kid's a super, I'm tellin' ya, Dale, a super." Brown was definitely interested.

"Can you get ahold of him?" he asked Parker.

"You kiddin', coach?" He picked up the phone and dialed the number. "Hey, Bernard there? Out? What you mean out? Hey, tell him Rodney called. I'll get him later."

The day had zoomed by quickly. It was close to 8 P.M. when Brown, Schaffel, the reporter, and Angelo Whitcover, a salesman for Pro Keds who had lent Brown his car for the day, headed out for dinner at a steakhouse near Schaffel's office. Parker was invited, but said he had other plans, though he walked over to the restaurant, came inside, and devoured several rolls before leaving for the night.

"You'll get in touch with Bernard, right?" Brown asked before Parker left.

"Don't worry, coach. He'll know you're coming."

Over a leisurely dinner, Schaffel and Whitcover occasionally teased Brown about being too clean, too straight, too morally righteous ever to win a national championship. But it was obvious they held their friend in high esteem. The same could not be said of their feelings for many of his colleagues.

"It's getting worse every year, I'm convinced of it," said Schaffel. "There's some real pirates out there, nothing but dirty stinking thieves. They'll rob these kids blind."

Schaffel recently had been involved in a bad run-in with

the Houston coach, Guy Lewis, over a player named Michael Lawrence, who worked in his office. Lawrence did not play high school basketball, but Schaffel had helped him try out for a United States youth team that would be touring Europe in the summer of 1973.

The tryout was held at Indiana State University in Terre Haute, and a number of college coaches, including Houston's Lewis, attended. Lawrence played sensationally, and Lewis told him he would like to have him come to Houston the next fall on scholarship. But in order to graduate from high school on time, Lawrence would have had to attend summer school. In order to attend summer school, he would have had to give up the European tour. He decided to go on the tour, told Lewis he would graduate the following January and still wanted to come to Houston. Would that be all right? he asked the coach. Of course, Lewis told him.

As the fall of his senior year in high school dragged on, Lawrence talked incessantly about going to Houston. All his friends knew about it, and he was treated with new-found respect everywhere he went. But Houston stopped writing to Michael Lawrence. In fact, Schaffel said, he never heard from the school again. No mail. No telegrams. No calls. Schaffel tried to reach Lewis, but was never able to get through. Finally, Schaffel wrote the coach a letter, telling him how disgusted he was with the Houston way of doing things. He also told Lawrence to forget about the school. "It was heartbreaking," he said. "That's the only place that kid wanted to go, and they dumped him." Lawrence wound up playing at Washington State; Lewis and Houston wound up on Schaffel's blacklist.

Shortly after 11 P.M. dinner was over, and Whitcover drove Brown to his hotel near LaGuardia Airport in Queens. But the coach couldn't sleep. He stretched out on the bed, loosened his tie, and talked to the reporter until the early morning hours about college basketball, and what's wrong with it.

"Why do I want to make a commitment to college athletics? Do I want to become famous? Do I want to be Ralph Nader or somebody? No. I want to try—and this sounds awfully pied piper—I would like to try and save college athletics.

"But I can't get people to speak up. They're afraid. Now look, I could care less about some of these things—you're on a guy's campus and he gets your teeth fixed or gives you a winter coat or a pair of shoes. I'm talking about the big things, the things that distort a kid's values.

"Hey, we're gonna fly up our own rear ends pretty soon. I've told the people in the NCAA that hell, they're looking for a damned needle in a haystack. Forget about that, burn the book, and concentrate on three major rules. You can't give a kid a car, you can't give a kid a lot of money, or you can't change his grades to get him in school or eligible. Those are the kinds of rules I don't want to see broken.

"The whole idea about athletics, the whole concept, it's been completely 100 per cent turned around. You cheat to get kids in and then you can't discipline those kids. You'll almost get a standing ovation when you fall on the floor for a loose ball, which is a sad commentary on the 1970s.

"I've heard guys at conventions, they'll be tapping another guy on the back and saying things like 'Well, I bought me three or four niggers. You can buy niggers off.'

"Hey, these kids have got to tell that guy 'Screw you.' If that guy is gonna lay money on the line with cold cash or buy you, he's challenging your dignity, he's telling you what he thinks of you."

Brown talked at length about Mickey Heard, a gifted

player from New Haven, Connecticut, who just completed his sophomore year at LSU.

"Mickey told me that one southern school offered to plant someone in the city for him to take his tests. They offered him $1,000 in cash if he'd sign. They offered him an automobile when he arrived. They offered his mother $350 a month and him $250 a month. I asked him if that's what he wants to be, a purchased athlete, or what. No, he didn't. He came to LSU, for nothing. His grades weren't good enough so we couldn't get him a scholarship. He came down this last summer, and I worked him in 11 different jobs so he could pay for his own way in the fall.

"When Mickey got to school, I noticed he was extremely shy, didn't communicate real well. I bet he isn't a real good reader, I said to myself. I tested him. You know what his reading level was? 3.5. I just died. I couldn't believe this. Third grade, fifth month.

"Well, we put two doctors on him, two full-time doctors in special education to work with him on phonics and flash cards and all kinds of machines. For the first time in his life, he could read a magazine.

"He came to my office and said to me, 'Coach, do you really think that I can be a pro basketball player?' I said, 'Mickey, there's no question in my mind.' 'Oh, coach, I hope so,' he said, 'because I want to go back to New Haven and I want to talk to the Board of Education and I want to tell them about the teachers in the schools that just sit up there and smoke and have recess and don't teach the people how to read or anything.'

"This is an unbelievable case history, yet here's a guy that could have easily destroyed his whole life. But he's gonna do just fine now, just fine. And he won't be corrupted."

Brown was up shortly before eight the next morning and,

after a shower and shave, was back on the telephone. Scheduled for the day were trips to four of New York City's five boroughs, and the coach did not particularly feel like driving all those places himself. He tried calling a friend on Long Island who had once offered to drive him around whenever he came to the area, but he had already left for work, his wife said, and probably couldn't be reached until after lunch.

Another thought came upon him. A taxicab. "Why not pay a cabbie $50 to take us around all day?" A few minutes later Brown was heading for LaGuardia Airport, several blocks from the Hotel. At the terminal some 25 taxis were lined up, waiting to pick up passengers supplied by the dispatcher. Brown walked up to a cab in the middle of the line and made his pitch. The cabbie wanted $60, and after a brief discussion Brown had his chauffeur.

Brown's first stop that day was smack in the middle of the Bedford-Stuyvesant section of Brooklyn, an area considered to be among the worst ghettos in America. He went to a sporting-goods store operated by a group known as Bedford-Stuyvesant Sports Unlimited. The store's proprietor, Lester Roberts, coached Bernard King in several neighborhood leagues.

"You know Bernard King pretty well, Lester, don't you?" Roberts nodded yes. "Listen, do you think he'd mind if I came over to talk to him? He's just the kind of kid we need."

"Sure, coach, I'll call him and tell him you're coming." Roberts picked up the telephone and spoke with King briefly. "Now just stay until Coach Brown gets there, all right? He'll be over in a couple of hours."

Brown stayed at the store a few minutes longer. He bought a T-shirt for his daughter, was introduced to several clerks, and even had time to recommend a brand of sneakers to a youngster who had wandered in off the street with a fistful of money.

"I understand Bernard's playing in a game over at Pace tonight," he said to Roberts.

"No, coach, he's not gonna be there. He goes to school at night so he can graduate on time. He won't be playing, but there's some other pretty good kids."

"Well, we better get over to see him," said Brown. On the way, however, the coach wanted to make two stops, both to visit parents of players he had recruited for Utah State.

Brown stopped briefly at the apartment of Mr. and Mrs. Walter Bees, a few blocks from Sports Unlimited. Six men stood on the stoop, blocking his entrance to the building, but Brown charged through. "Looks like a cop," said one. "Nah, his suit's pressed," said another.

The Bees lived in a comfortable four-room apartment, though every few minutes the place shook from the vibrations of the subway trains that passed by overhead a block away. They were surprised to see Brown that day but were thoroughly delighted. Brown had recruited their son, Walter, Jr., to Utah State in 1967. Junior was 6-foot-10 and a high school All-America. He stayed in Utah for two years, suffered a serious knee injury, then failed out and came back to Bedford-Stuyvesant.

"I will never forget that day you came in here and made Walter go back to school," said Mrs. Bees, a large, pleasant woman with an Ultrabrite smile. Indeed, Bees had been moping around his parents' apartment after flunking out of school. He had no job, and he was miserable.

"Mr. Brown came in here one day and got really angry at Walter," Mrs. Bees recalled. "He said he wasn't leaving the apartment until Walter made up his mind that he was going back to school. Walter needed that."

Brown made arrangements for Bees to attend Minot

State, his old school, on a basketball scholarship, and Bees enrolled the next fall. He played for two years and graduated last June. "Mr. Brown saved that boy's life," said Mr. Bees, who let his wife do most of the talking.

By the time Brown left, the stoop-sitters had decided to go elsewhere. Brown made one more stop, to visit the parents of Marvin Roberts, another of his former Utah State players, before he finally pointed the cabbie in the direction of Bernard King's apartment.

Bernard King answered the door. He was at least 6-foot-5, and was wearing a T-shirt, jeans, and a pair of white hightop basketball shoes. He ushered Brown into the dining room and sat down.

"Now Bernard, I don't want to take too much of your time," Brown said, "so I'll make it quick." He immediately launched into his presentation. It was basically the same pitch he had given the day before in Mrs. Green's living room. This time, Brown put a heavy emphasis on the fact that he had sent five players to the professionals, and King seemed extremely interested. But he rarely said a word.

Halfway through the conversation, Bernard's mother walked through the door. She was tall like her son, and when she smiled her teeth jutted out of her mouth in every direction. She was extremely shy, and like Mrs. Green seemed flustered to have this tall white stranger in her home. She quickly excused herself, saying, "I've got some things to do in the kitchen," but out of sight she listened to every word.

When Brown was through, he walked into the living room, and Mrs. King came in, too. Trophies were everywhere. Bernard's. His little brother, Al's. And some belonging to his older brother, who played basketball at West Virginia Wesleyan.

"You've got a wonderful young man there, Mrs. King, you must be very proud of him," Brown said.

"Yes, I am," she answered. "What school you say you were from?"

"Louisiana State. That's in Baton Rouge, real close to New Orleans."

"Oh, yeah, I heard of that. Well you know I'm not going to have anything to do with Bernard's decision. It's completely up to Bernard. It's his choice. I'll go along with anything he decides."

Since this was Brown's first meeting with King, he played it extremely low-keyed. He merely wondered if Bernard were interested in visiting the LSU campus, and when he shook his head, yes, the coach said he would call him later in the week and arrange a date.

When Brown left the apartment he was ecstatic. "Did you see the eye-contact when I was talking to Bernard?" he said. "I think he's really interested. And his mother was right. She's not going to have anything to do with his decision.

"But I thought he was really receptive. He never even met me before, but he was friendly and relaxed. The only thing that bothers me is that we're getting involved with him pretty late. But it's worth the chance.

"Why did I talk so much about the pro business? Well, you've got to. Kids want to know about things like that. And in Bernard's case, I think he has a good chance to play pro ball someday. I don't want to give these kids false hopes. But if Bernard King comes to LSU and does well, people are going to see him play. He is a legitimate pro prospect."

The basketball game that night was a complete waste of

time, though the Russians had a 6-5 center who showed some promise. He was unavailable, however.

Back in the hotel room, Brown decided to change his itinerary. He had been planning to go to Pittsburgh the next morning to visit Harold Johnson, a junior college prospect, but he had called Johnson earlier in the day and was told that he wasn't interested. So Brown decided instead to go right on to Baltimore to speak with Leon Love, a 6-foot-8 player from Bay Junior College, who had averaged 18 points and 19 rebounds a game the previous season.

Brown was on the 9 A.M. shuttle to Washington, where the reporter's car was parked. They drove up to Baltimore, and arrived at Bay College—the entire school is housed in a former office building smack in the middle of the city—shortly before 11:30 A.M.

Brown had called ahead, and he went immediately to the office of Coach George Milby, a gregarious fellow who had come to Baltimore two years before when John F. Kennedy College in Omaha, Nebraska, had dropped its basketball program for lack of funds. All of his players at Bay College had been recruited off Baltimore's playgrounds. All of them were black.

Love entered the office a few minutes later. He was wearing a stunning open-necked shirt that was beige in front, and decorated with a likeness of a bare-breasted black woman on the back. He had just that morning returned from a recruiting trip to Tennessee. Milby introduced him to Brown.

"Oh wow, LSU," he gushed. "Man, I heard a lot about your school. And you say you're the head coach at LSU. Oh wow.

"I just got back from Tennessee, man, and it was terrible. I was there four days, and I never even saw the head coach. I was alone most of the time, and I didn't dig that. Then they showed me their offense, man. It was too slow for me. I'm crossing them off my list. It was bad, really bad, man."

"I'm sorry to hear that," Brown said with as straight a face as possible. "I haven't seen you play, Leon, but my assistant has, and he's really impressed with you. He said you can really help our program."

With that, Brown was off and pitching. Milby stayed in the room and read the morning Baltimore *Sun* as Brown talked for 30 minutes about his background, his program, his school, and his success with sending players to the professionals.

He also told Leon that an alumnus in Washington, D.C., could get him a summer job at $5 an hour working in a recreation program. "Are you interested in visiting, Leon?" Brown asked.

"Oh wow, yeah," Leon said. "How about this weekend, coach?"

"Now Leon," Milby interrupted, "I don't want you missing any more classes. You know that lady's gonna flunk you if you miss too many of her classes."

"Don't worry, coach, I'll be back. If I leave Friday afternoon, I can do it."

At that point, the phone in Milby's office rang. It was Press Maravich, the coach at Appalachian State and the man Brown had replaced at LSU. "Tell him I'm not here," Leon asked Milby, and the coach complied, telling Maravich to call later in the day.

Love had to leave. The Tennessee assistant coach, Marty Morriss, had flown back to Baltimore with him from Knoxville, and was waiting in a restaurant down the block to take Love to lunch.

"That's all right, Leon, go ahead," Brown assured him.

"I wish I didn't have to go, coach, I'd rather sit here and talk with you, but I got to."

Love left, and a few minutes later Brown was heading for the door. "Wait a second, coach, I'd like you to meet someone," Milby interrupted, introducing Brown to a Bay College official who also happened to be an LSU alumnus.

"Yes sir, coach, Leon is a wonderful boy," he said. "I also think he's going to be greatly influenced by his father." In fact, before he had left Milby's office, Love had called his father and repeated his sad story about the Tennessee trip.

Brown was intrigued. "Can I meet his father?" he asked Milby.

Fortunately, Leon happened to stroll back in the office, and was only too happy to call his father back. "Dad, there's somebody I want you to meet. He's the LSU coach, and they're real interested in me."

An hour later, Brown was standing in Cookie's Connection, a clothing store off Baltimore's Pennsylvania Avenue. Mr. Love, a salesman, was busy with a customer, but finally broke loose.

"Can we go somewhere and talk?" Brown asked Love, a nattily dressed fellow who took 10 minutes to adjust his tie before leaving the shop with the coach.

Love took Brown to the Club Riviera, a dimly lit bar in the heart of Baltimore's black business district. As the Temptations blared out of the juke box, Brown ordered a Budweiser, Mr. Love scotch and water. Then they talked.

Mr. Love said he was very interested in seeing that his son received a good education, and very impressed by the fact that Tennessee would provide tutors for his boy at no cost.

"Well, Mr. Love, every school will do that for him," explained Brown. "Did you know at LSU we have the only full-time academic counselor for athletes in our conference?"

Mr. Love smiled. "No, I didn't. That's good to hear."

Brown also mentioned the $5 an hour job, the fact that LSU athletes earned every penny they got. "I'm not going to come here and buy your boy," Brown said. "I don't believe in that. Once you buy a kid, he won't respect you and he won't play for you."

Love, Jr., had already received several illegal offers. A Florida school had offered to give his girl friend a scholarship and get his father a job if he enrolled. Another coach offered his coach, Milby, $5,000 if he could convince Love and Harold Johnson of Pittsburgh to go to his school.

"Well yes, coach, I know what you mean," Mr. Love said. "I always brought my kids up never to take something for nothing. I never did when I was a kid. I've had to work hard for everything I got. I work two jobs. I work my ass off, and nobody's gonna buy my boy."

After an hour and another round of drinks, Brown drove Mr. Love back to work and left Baltimore. "I've got a good feeling about Leon Love," he said, often.

The next morning, Brown flew back to Baton Rouge. It had been an extremely successful three days, and he was confident that all three players would at least visit LSU. He also was almost certain that one of the three would be playing on his team the following year.

Classes began at LSU on August 26, 1974, but Al Green, Bernard King, and Leon Love were not enrolled, though Green wanted desperately to come. He wound up at Arizona Western Junior College in Yuma, however, and King and Love would be teammates, for awhile, at Tennessee.

Green had made up his mind to attend LSU during his visit to the campus, he says, the last of 16 he made to schools around the country. "My father's parents live down there, you know," he says. "My father doesn't live at home, but we're still pretty tight.

"When I was down at Baton Rouge, I talked to my grandparents and all my other relatives. I got uncles and aunts living down there. They said coach Brown was for real. They really love him down there.

"Nobody else influenced my decision. Lewie [Schaffel] told me I couldn't go wrong with Dale, and so did Rodney Parker. Parker's a straight dude. I trust him. He was out to help me, and he did."

Green had narrowed his choices to LSU and Bowling Green in Ohio before finally making his decision. Why Bowling Green? "They had a 7-foot dude, he's a good rebounder, and their other guard wasn't so good," he says. "I could have averaged 30 points a game there. They said I could shoot it when I got it."

But Al Green could not have gone to Bowling Green or LSU, or anywhere, really, because he did not have enough credits to graduate from high school, and technically was not eligible to attend an NCAA school.

However, there are ways to get around that sticky detail. The NCAA allows youngsters in Green's situation to take the national GED, or high school equivalency test. In order to be eligible for admission to an NCAA school a score of 43.6 must be obtained.

Brown, who did not know Green would not graduate when he recruited him in April, spent the early part of the summer trying to find a place where Green could take the test. "It was bizarre, some of the rules about who could take the test, where they could take it," Brown said. "In New York we found out he couldn't take it until he was 21 and out of school for a year. In Louisiana there was a residency rule, and in Idaho it was the same thing. We finally had him take it in Arizona."

And Al Green failed, by nine points.

"He was coming here, it was a locked case," Brown said

one day last September. "It was an amazing thing, because some schools told Al not to even worry about the test. They'd get someone to pass it for him, or do something.

"But I talked him out of doing it illegally, and I feel a little bit guilty about it. I just told him it's your decision but I recommend that you do it honorably.

"He studied all summer, worked his rear end off trying to pass that test, and then he flunks it." Even after receiving the news that Green had failed the test, Brown recommended that he come to Baton Rouge, get a job, and play for the local AAU team while finishing up the credits to graduate from high school.

"It would have meant sitting out a year of college basketball and Al wanted to play," Brown said, "so he enrolled at Arizona Western. He'd have to play there for two years before he came to LSU, but I don't think he will. It's such a shame. We wanted him, he wanted us, and he'll probably never get here.

"He's a great kid, and I feel a personal responsibility to him. But even if he doesn't come here, in the end I think he'll like himself a whole lot better because he did it the right way."

Bernard King never really considered LSU. Just as Brown feared, he had entered the picture rather late, and it cost him. King never visited LSU's campus. Less than a month after Brown left his Brooklyn apartment, he signed to play at Tennessee.

"LSU was too late," King says. "I liked the coach, but I had never even heard from him before that day in the apartment, and that was April already. I had decided pretty much to go to Tennessee back then. Those people treated me real nice. They didn't hang on me. When I was down there, they let me talk to whoever I wanted to. They let me find out things for myself. And I did.

"They got some nice players coming in there, too. That dude Love, a 7-footer from Philadelphia. I'm really happy about going down there." So was Tennessee. In his first game as a freshman, King scored 42 points.

Leon Love had the most difficult time making his final decision. Even before he had visited LSU's campus, he had told South Florida coach Bill Gibson he would be coming to his school in the fall.

The day Love returned from his visit to LSU, Gibson met him at Dulles Airport in suburban Virginia as he was changing planes for a flight to Baltimore. The coach had been waiting for Love at the Bay College office when the youngster called to tell his coach, Milby, when he would be back in school.

As soon as he heard the flight number, Gibson was out the door and headed for the airport, more than 90 miles away. He caught Love in the terminal and the youngster assured him that he was still coming to South Florida. But he still was not ready to sign a national letter-of-intent.

When he arrived back in Baltimore, Love was met at Friendship Airport by Morriss, the Tennessee assistant. Morriss, in fact, had been in Baltimore the better part of two weeks trying to persuade Love to come to Knoxville. The next day Tennessee's head coach, Ray Mears, flew in, and Morriss, Love, his father, and the head coach went over to a local Holiday Inn for "a discussion."

The session lasted from 7:30 P.M. until about 1:00 the next morning, at which time sleepy Leon Love decided that perhaps it was in his best interests to attend Tennessee after all.

"They pulled out all the stops," said Milby. "They had a brochure of the team with a two-page spread on Leon they had done up, a big picture of him jumping up toward the rim. They got him a job if he wants it in Knoxville with some alumnus." Tennessee also agreed to give a scholarship to Donnie Evans, a guard at Bay College whom Love later described as "my main man."

Love's father said Tennessee "was the best school for him. I liked the coach, he's one of the best in the country. You know their assistant coach stayed around here about two weeks. We went to dinner a couple of times, had a few drinks together."

"I tell you," Leon, Jr., said, "my father wanted me to go to Tennessee, and I love my father and I listen to my father. We both decided it would be the best thing for me.

"Yeah, man, they put some heavy pressure on me. That night in the hotel was something else. I don't like being hassled. I kind of wanted to talk to LSU once more before I made up my mind, but I didn't, and it's too late to do anything about it.

"But LSU, oh wow, what a great place. The trip was a groove all the way. I met the nicest people. Not just the girls. They left me alone, no dates, nothing like that. I walked around campus on Friday. It was a regular school day, and things were really together down there. Tennessee called me twice while I was there. It didn't bother me too much. I was having too good a time.

"I got a friend, Marvin Payne, goes to Edmonson High School in Baltimore. He's 6-8, 225, and he's young. I'm gonna try to talk him into going to LSU, 'cause I really liked that place.

"I don't want to say I made a mistake, but it's always gonna be on my mind whether I should have gone to LSU. If it was up to me, I would have gone there. But Tennessee talked to my father more than they did me. You know how those things work out, man. I wanted to give everybody a fair shake. I dug Coach Gibson and I dug Coach Brown, they were together people. I hope I'll like it at Tennessee."

Still, Love had a severe case of the second thoughts. Two weeks before classes were to have started at Tennessee, Love and his main man, Evans, left Knoxville and told some of their friends they were not coming back.

"Leon called me and told me he just didn't like it there," Milby said. "I don't know where he is."

There were rumors that he and Evans had talked to the people at Fayetteville State in North Carolina and also at South Florida. Both schools do not honor the national letter-of-intent, and could have accepted the two players.

Then, a week before classes were to begin, Love and Evans arrived back in Knoxville, after still another change of heart.

"Yeah, they went back," Milby confirmed, "but who the hell knows how long they'll stay?"

It was not very long at all. In mid-November, both players had dropped out of school.

"Leon never even told us he was leaving," said Stu Aberdeen, a Tennessee assistant.

"Donnie went with him. Whatever Leon did, Donnie did, too. He [Love] had some problems. For one thing, he got sick. He wasn't in very good shape. He wasn't going to classes and I think he saw he wasn't going to play for us."

Why did Tennessee spend so much time and effort to get him there?

"Oh, you never know about those kind of things," Aberdeen said. "At the time, we thought he could help us. Leon just wasn't good enough. No, I don't know where he is now [December 1974]. I know he's not in school. It's just one of those things."

7 / The Parents

A TREE GROWS in the Brooklyn backyard of Mrs. Ethel Roberts. It is an oak, she thinks, but it doesn't really matter. She is content to know that it is simply there, along with her roses, a few scraggly shrubs, and a patch of grass.

For 22 years, Mrs. Roberts and her husband, Leroy, lived in the Crown Heights section of Brooklyn, in the projects, where winos defecated in the elevators and children could not tell the difference between rats and alleycats. Her apartment was cramped, though spotlessly clean, even if the halls did stink of urine, vomit, and the ammonia used to stifle the previous two stenches. For years, Mrs. Roberts looked out her window and saw nothing but asphalt, the building across the way, or occasionally a mugging.

Mr. and Mrs. Roberts also had a son. He was lean and tall and grew up to stand 6-foot-8 in his stocking feet. He could also perform wonderful feats with a basketball. His

name was Marvin, and when he was 17 he played for
Wingate High, a few blocks away.

From all across America in 1967, coaches came to see
Mr. and Mrs. Roberts. Many seemed rather nervous, tense,
knowing full well that few white men had ever set foot in
this sorry section of the ghetto. Dale Brown, however,
brought his wife and little daughter, and no coach had ever
done that before.

Brown then was a young, energetic assistant at Utah
State, and he was looking for players. He had read about
Roberts in Howard Garfinkel's report, which called him
"the sleeper of the year" in the class of 1967.

Mr. and Mrs. Roberts got along famously with Brown,
his wife, Vonnie, and four-year-old Robyn. They also liked
what Brown had to say to their son. He told Marvin that if
he came west to Utah State and did well enough, the
professional scouts would know all about him. They would
offer him a lot of money, and with it he could move his
parents out of the projects, into their own home, with grass
and trees and no one to hassle them about the rent.

Mr. and Mrs. Roberts were pleased. For every son who
can shoot the 15-foot jumper, dribble a ball through his legs
without breaking stride, and throw the outlet pass 50 feet
down court there exists a mother and father who dream that
one day their boy can be photographed next to his $30,000
Rolls Royce, just like Walt Frazier.

They should know better. Less than one per cent of all
the seniors now playing basketball in America's 22,000
private and public high schools will ever make it to the
professional ranks. In 1973 there were 5,700 college seniors
playing basketball, and the professionals signed only 55 of
them to contracts.

But the Roberts family knew nothing about those statistics. They knew only that they enjoyed being with Coach

Brown. He told them what they wanted to hear. And more important: "Coach Brown didn't seem like a person who was prejudiced," Mrs. Roberts said.

"I liked the way he sounded," Marvin Roberts added. "I thought he was an honest guy."

So he went to Utah State. Oh, he had his occasional problems there. The school is located in a hotbed of the Mormon church, and Roberts found out quickly that Mormons "dug black dudes, as long as you were a good black dude and didn't bother their daughters. As long as you played ball you were all right." Roberts started for three years at Utah State, and when he was finished the Denver Rockets made him their No. 2 choice in the 1971 draft. He signed a three-year contract for $500,000.

That same year, Marvin Roberts took a chunk of that money and moved his mother and father out of the Sterling Place apartment, out of the projects, and over to 36 East 58th Street, a neighborhood that was mostly white—part Italian, part Jewish.

"I love this little house," Mrs. Roberts told a visitor. "This is what Marvin wanted to do for his mama and his papa. Everything happened just like Coach Brown said it would. I'm not sure I believed it all back then. But now, this is a dream come true."

Virginia Dantley had heard all the pitches and promises from America's brightest—and brashest—college basketball coaches, and she said, shortly before the recruiting ordeal of her son was finally over, "I sympathize with all of them. I wish I had seven sons."

But she had only one, Adrian Dantley, a 6-foot-5, 220-pound bundle of brute basketball brawn, and the real object of all the attention and flattery, letters and telephone calls that regularly came her way.

Mrs. Dantley became impressed by some, particularly Maryland's Lefty Driesell, a man she once described as having the ability "to charm the birds right out of the trees."

He also left her and Adrian thoroughly flabbergasted that night when he came into the living room of her comfortable Southwest Washington apartment and, for the grand finale of his presentation, whipped out his school's uniform—warmup jacket, game shirt, even the short pants, all with the name "Dantley" neatly stitched on.

"It was perfectly legal," says Morgan Wootten, Dantley's high school coach, "but that was the first time I've ever come across that particular tactic. The man meant business."

Still, Mrs. Dantley was not at all turned off by Driesell or any of the other coaches she met in perhaps the most tumultuous year of her life. "They're all so nice and sincere," she said, even the coach who claimed he had lost five pounds worrying about Adrian's final decision.

Indeed, parents are recruited almost as heavily as their talented offspring, for all the obvious reasons. And, though most parents insist they do not try to influence their sons' final selection, they simply cannot help but play a major role.

Tom McMillen's decision to attend the University of Maryland was based, to a great extent, on the adverse effect another choice might have had on his family.

"The only thing that kept Tom McMillen from going to North Carolina was the respect he had for his parents," says Rich Miller, McMillen's high school coach in Mansfield, Pennsylvania.

"I got caught up in the whole thing," says McMillen, a 6-foot-11 high school All-America and the most heavily recruited player in the class of 1970, a year that also saw one Bill Walton graduate from a San Diego high school.

"My brother Jay played at Maryland," says McMillen. "My mother knew Bill Gibson [then the Virginia coach] very well. My father liked Coach Driesell because they're both very competitive types. I was leaning toward Coach [Dean] Smith [of North Carolina]. I had a sister at Pennsylvania, and she was pushing that. There were a million different things I was being crowded into. I had no one to turn to."

At one point, the pressure became so great, McMillen admits, that "I almost had a nervous breakdown."

McMillen is one of five children, the son of the late Dr. James McMillen, a prosperous Mansfield dentist. His brother Jay had played basketball at Maryland from 1965 to 1967, and one of Jay's teammates was Joe Harrington, an assistant coach at Maryland during Tom's senior year in high school. And oh, what a year it was.

McMillen averaged 47.7 points a game and 22 rebounds. He was president of the student body, valedictorian of the senior class, a prize-winning debater, and an altar boy. In his four years at Mansfield High, he scored 3,068 points, an average of 35.3 a game.

By April 1970 it became apparent that three schools— Maryland, North Carolina, and Virginia—were still in the running to sign the most highly recruited athlete in America. On April 11 he gave the three head coaches a chance to make a final pitch. On April 13 he went into seclusion, and the next day he apparently was ready to decide.

He called Miller, his high school coach, and the two went for a 45-minute drive through the hilly roads around the northern Pennsylvania town. "Tommy was very upset," Miller recalls. "A few times he'd say, 'You pick the school for me, coach, I can't decide.' I just kept telling him, 'It's your choice, go where you'll be happiest.'

"After a while he said, 'Let's go make the call.' He called up Dean Smith from my house and said he was coming."

Smith later described the conversation. "He kind of talked around the thing," Smith said. "Finally he said, 'Coach Smith, how would I look in Carolina blue?' My wife saw me getting visibly excited and she started jumping up and down.

"Tom told me that he wanted me to contact Jack Williams [North Carolina's sports publicist] immediately to release the fact that he would sign with us. I called Jack, and the story broke minutes later."

Smith and McMillen decided they would hold a press conference the next day at Pierce's Restaurant in Elmira, New York, 20 miles north of Mansfield. A friend owned the place and had promised McMillen the use of his facilities when the youngster finally made up his mind.

McMillen, quite obviously, was elated, and Miller drove him back home and left him off at the front door, not bothering to get out of the car. "I figured it would be better if he went in alone," he said.

It wasn't. McMillen's parents were not pleased. His mother still favored Gibson, his father and brother Driesell, and McMillen's elation soon turned to despair. He felt he had hurt his parents deeply, and spent that night in sleepless agony.

"I had emotional attachments," he says. "I was pulled 100 different ways." Thus began what McMillen now describes as "one of the worst days of my life."

The next morning, McMillen changed his mind again. He called Chapel Hill from school to tell Smith not to come, but the coach and his staff already were in the air. McMillen called the restaurant and canceled the press conference. He called his parents and told them about his change of heart.

"Now, I don't know how this happened, but my brother and Joe Harrington also heard about it [the decision to attend North Carolina], and they came up to Mansfield. Gibson came up, too. In fact, I was walking out the door of the high school and I ran into him.

"I broke down. My high school principal got me out of there. I went to his house in the mountains, just to get away from them all. So Gibson, my brother, and Joe Harrington and all the North Carolina people were in town, and I was nowhere to be found."

"I gave Tom the key to my house and told him to drive his car into my garage so no one would know he was there," says Ted Besanceney, Mansfield High principal. "I also told him that whenever I had a problem, I went for a walk in the woods. We've got about 150 acres three miles outside of town. It's very peaceful, very relaxing."

It was, until McMillen got lost in the woods and was chased by a dog—obviously not the woodsman he was the basketball player. "It was getting dark," McMillen recalls, "so I went down to the nearest light I could see down in the valley. As I was walking up to the house with the light on, there's Joe Harrington, standing right there. I just said, 'Joe, take me back to Mr. Besanceney's house.' He didn't say a word, and neither did I. He just dropped me off and left." Meanwhile, Miller and Besanceney explained McMillen's predicament to the other coaches, and they finally left town.

Between mid-April and mid-June, all three head coaches kept in touch with McMillen and his family, "although Dr. and Mrs. McMillen became increasingly cold toward me," Smith said. Mrs. McMillen especially resented Smith's presence in her son's life, though Smith never really was quite sure why.

On June 23 McMillen called Smith and told him he was ready to sign. Smith again went to Mansfield the next day, and met McMillen at Pierce's. Once more McMillen announced he would attend North Carolina, this time on a special athletic-academic scholarship. It was not an athletic grant-in-aid and did not require the approval of his parents.

On June 25 Dr. McMillen placed a telephone call to Ladd Baucam, sports editor of the Greensboro, North Carolina, *Record.* Dr. McMillen said the family was "grief-stricken" over his son's decision to attend Carolina, charged that Smith had usurped their authority as parents, and said that recruiting was "a nasty dirty business."

"Not a member of our family wants him to go to North Carolina," Dr. McMillen told Baucam, who was more than willing to print every word.

But on June 30 Dr. McMillen insisted that "a minor misunderstanding" had been "ironed out" and "the family now realizes that North Carolina is the best place for our son." The next day Smith wrote the McMillens a letter saying he was pleased with their change in attitude toward him and the school.

"I received a return letter from Mrs. McMillen which indicated that they were still very much opposed to me personally and to North Carolina," Smith said, adding that from that point until early August he had serious difficulty contacting McMillen by telephone in Mansfield.

On August 7, Smith said, he received an angry call from Mrs. McMillen over a letter her son had received from someone named Mike Johnston, who identified himself as president of the "Tar Heel Club" in Chapel Hill. The letter informed McMillen he would have several credit cards and a $100 a month stipend, once he arrived in Chapel Hill. But there was no Mike Johnston listed in the Chapel Hill telephone book. A Tar Heel Club was listed in Durham, North Carolina, but the name of Mike Johnston did not appear on its membership list. Smith said he had no idea who sent the letter, and insisted he had never heard of Mike Johnston.

After that, McMillen was thoroughly confused. At one point, Virginia even seemed to be leading. But he was not firmly committed, and would not make up his mind until September, until the final day of registration at all three schools. At that point, his brother Jay played the most crucial role.

"I went over to the McMillens the night before Tom was going to leave for school," Rich Miller says. "Bill Gibson was in the living room playing cards with Tom's folks. Tom was packing upstairs, but he still didn't know where he'd be packing for. That same night, his brother Jay came up, and they went out for a drive.

"I didn't see Tom until the next morning [September 10], when he came over to the high school to say good-bye. I guess it was about 8:30. I remember thinking, They'll have to drive like hell to make it to North Carolina before registration closes."

But there was no chance of that. McMillen had already wired Smith, who was in Europe conducting a clinic. "Coach Smith," the telegram read, "going to Maryland for reasons you know."

"Tommy said, 'I'm going to Maryland,' " Miller recalls. "Jay just smiled. And then, they were gone."

Four years later McMillen insisted, "I'm not one to regret things. I ended up here, and it hasn't been a bad decision." Indeed, McMillen was named three times to All-America teams, set a school scoring record, won a Rhodes scholarship, and was a No. 1 pick of the Buffalo Braves in the 1974 draft. (He chose the Rhodes scholarship and a two-year no-cut contract for an estimated $250,000 to play for an Italian team.)

But his decision was based in large part on the not-so-subtle influence of his family. And most coaches know that if they can win over the parents, final victory—the signing of a son—is close at hand.

"They tell you everything you want to hear," says Butch Lee, a blue-chip guard from Harlem in the high school class of 1974. "If I tell a recruiter I'm interested in mathematics, he tells me, oh, they have a great math department. I tell another recruiter I'm interested in business, and they tell me how good their business department is. No matter what it is that I want to major in, their schools have the best department."

Mrs. Mildred Buckley put one recruiter into a state of semi-shock when she asked him what provisions his school made for advanced standing, a program in which a high school student can bypass certain required freshman courses by taking a test.

"The guy didn't know," Mrs. Buckley says. "It was kind of funny because he looked so embarrassed. But before we left that day, we got an answer."

The University of Virginia, in fact, aware of McMillen's interest in pursuing a premedical course, arranged to have him view a knee operation at the university hospital when he arrived on campus to visit. "He watched it all," says Dr. Frank McCue, an orthopedic surgeon who performed the operation, "and after it was over he asked some of the most intelligent questions I've ever heard a layman ask about surgical procedure. He impressed me as a brilliant kid."

Every mother appreciates knowing her son will be well taken care of when she's not around, and Mrs. John Gilheany, the mother of De Matha All-America Bill

Langloh, a teammate of Dantley's, had to be impressed with the gushing concern of Duke coach Bucky Waters.

The coach had come up to De Matha to talk with Langloh the same day the 6-foot-3 guard was scheduled to take a private plane to visit the Furman campus in South Carolina.

According to several witnesses in the gym that day, Waters told Mrs. Gilheany he had heard numerous radio reports of heavy thunder and lightning in the very same area Billy's plane would be heading. Wouldn't it be wise to postpone the trip, at least until the weather improved, he implored.

"He was so sincere you couldn't believe it," says one witness. "There was no way Bucky Waters wanted Bill Langloh visiting anywhere, unless of course it happened to be Duke." As it turned out, Waters shouldn't have been that concerned. Langloh went to Virginia, a two-hour drive from his house in suburban Maryland.

Dean Smith left a vivid impression on army Colonel and Mrs. William McCarthy of his concern for their son, Brendan, a high school All-America in football and basketball at De Matha in 1964. Colonel McCarthy, his wife, and seven of their nine children drove down to Chapel Hill while Brendan was being flown in from Washington in a private plane for his campus visit.

The family then planned to head over to High Point, North Carolina, where another son attended college. Brendan would fly back to Washington as scheduled, and take a taxi home. "But Dean Smith wouldn't hear of it," Colonel McCarthy says. "He told my wife that he would be at the airport in Washington to meet Brendan and take him home."

Late Sunday afternoon, Smith boarded a commercial flight from Greensboro and landed a few minutes before

McCarthy's private plane arrived at National Airport in Washington. He drove the 17-year-old high school senior to his Georgetown home, a $2 taxi ride and less than 15 minutes away from the terminal.

"Needless to say," Colonel McCarthy says, "we were very impressed." That entire weekend, in fact, was an unqualified success, even if Brendan did wind up attending Boston College, his father's alma mater, on a football scholarship.

"We got there [Chapel Hill] and there were two suites waiting for us and the children," Colonel McCarthy says. "There was Scotch and bourbon in our room, and about 20 minutes after we checked in, an assistant coach came by and we went out to a magnificent steak dinner.

"The next morning, we had a steak breakfast back at the athletes' dining room, then steak again for lunch. That night we went to an affair at the athletic director's house. They brought all the professors in, heads of departments and people like that. They do it very well. It made a lot of sense."

The campus visit now is more critical than ever before, especially since the NCAA in 1972 issued a new set of rules covering the entertainment of a prospect and his parents.

Before August 1, 1972, the wining and dining of recruits, their parents, and high school coaches went on in grand style. But now a coach supposedly is allowed to entertain only on his own campus. Not everyone follows the rules, of course, and restaurants with dark, dimly lit interiors get most of the business.

Occasionally, as Bob Cousy once found out, a parent would prefer cheesecake to steak. "You just keep pushing the buttons until you find what appeals to a kid, or to the kid's family," says Cousy, who for six years was head coach at Boston College before he left to coach in the NBA.

"I ran into one instance where Daddy-O came along [on a prospect's weekend visit to Chestnut Hill]. I was wondering why dad was so anxious to come until he came up to one of my people and asked if we could take him into town and take care of him. He was told we couldn't and he became quite indignant. He indicated this service had been provided for him on other visits."

Lonnie Perrin, a high school All-America running back from Washington, D.C., who wound up at Illinois, recalls one school's offer to move his mother out of their Northeast Washington tenement and into a new garden apartment. "They saw my mother, and all those kids, and they knew she was on social security," Perrin says. "When you're poor, they know what appeals to you."

Mrs. Wilma Robinson had more than an occasional unpleasant experience dealing with recruiters when her son, Wayne (Tree) Rollins, a 7-footer from Cordele, Georgia, was being actively pursued in 1972. "I wouldn't be a recruiter for nothing," she says. "It's a nasty job."

Mrs. Robinson is a staunch Baptist who serves as an instructor at a retardation center near her home. "It seemed like every time I drove home from work this guy was sitting out front in a new car," she recalls. "He said it would be Wayne's if he signed with them. I told him to take the cars away. If he brought one, he must have brought five.

"We'd go to bed with the phone ringing. It was always some coach. It was enough to drive a sane person right up the wall."

Yet many parents also admit the recruiting of their sons was a marvelous period in their lives, a time when they stopped being Mr. and Mrs. Smith and were introduced, instead, as the mother and father of Johnny (High School All-America) Smith.

"It was fabulous," says Colonel McCarthy. "My wife

always wanted to eat at the Sans Souci [Henry Kissinger's favorite Washington restaurant, and one of the more expensive spots in the nation's capital]. She was always reading that Jackie Kennedy ate there, and she wanted to try it. One day, the coach from LaSalle called and asked if we'd like to go out. 'Anywhere at all,' he said. So we picked the Sans Souci. We took some of the kids, Morgan Wootten and his wife, and Joe Kennedy [another De Matha player] and his folks—oh, about 13 or 14 of us. We opened the place and we closed the place; drinks before dinner, drinks after dinner, the whole works. LaSalle picked up the check. I hate to even think what it was."

Austin Carr, Sr., father of the Notre Dame All-America presently employed by the Cleveland Cavaliers, says his son frequently dined with recruiters at the Three Thieves restaurant in Washington, a most appropriately named spot.

"Those coaches had a convention at my house," Carr, Sr., a retired navy warehouse foreman, recalls. "They ran around like a bunch of flies.

"My son always had the same problem I had. I could never say no, and neither could he. Finally things were getting out of hand. He would have been gone on these trips every weekend, sometimes just for the sake of going. I finally had to make him narrow down his choices for visits. He picked Michigan, Syracuse, St. Bonaventure, Notre Dame, and North Carolina. Then we got it down to two, the last two, and that's when the serious business started."

Carr, Sr., favored North Carolina. He had been born and raised in the state, and Smith had made a favorable impression on him, as he usually does on parents. "We're still good friends," Carr, Sr., says. "He sends me Christmas cards, and calls up every now and then."

Carr, Jr., an All-America at Mackin High, leaned to

Notre Dame, and when his friends Sid Catlett of De Matha and Collis Jones of St. John's said they, too, were considering the South Bend school, he was sold. Almost.

"The day before we were going to announce the decision to go to Notre Dame—it was a Sunday as I recall," says Carr, Sr., "Austin got a call from Charlie Scott [then a North Carolina freshman and a widely publicized high-school player].

"Well, when Charlie hung up, Austin was almost in tears. He didn't know what to do or where to go. Son, I told him, whatever decision you make, I'll go along with it."

Carr, of course, wound up at Notre Dame, and so did his father "for as many games as I could get to see. I almost went broke seeing that boy play, but it was worth every dime." Still, Carr, Sr., could have saved considerable expenses had his son accepted an offer from any number of other schools.

"Some of them hinted they would pay our way out to see him play, two or three times a year, maybe more. One school offered to buy my younger boy one of those little motorcycles, you know, mini-bikes. Sure we could have had those kind of things.

"But I didn't want it. Why should I accept anything that could have jeopardized his career? There was money offered to him under the table, clothes and stuff like that. But he kept his nose clean. It was very hectic. The salesmanship was amazing. The recruiters keep constantly nagging you. You pick up the phone and it's a basketball coach.

"I tried to keep ones we weren't interested in from bothering Austin, but they always came up with these excuses to get to him. You can't stop people from calling. We had an unlisted number, but that didn't help. People can get your number."

Mrs. Dantley also had an unlisted number, though not by choice. Because of a mistake in the phone company records, her name never appeared in the directory, a blessing during her son's senior year. Adrian's paternal grandfather, Aaron Dantley, was listed, however, and received scads of calls from people hoping to gain a few words with his talented grandson.

Brendan McCarthy's mother knew that every Friday, shortly before noon, Johnny Ray, a Notre Dame assistant football coach, would call. "He asked one question every week," Mrs. McCarthy says. " 'Are we still in it?' That's all he wanted to know. Sometimes we talked about his kids, and my kids, small talk. They were always in it for football, so I always told him 'Yes, you're still in it.'

"When Brendan finally signed at Boston, I just dreaded that Friday phone call. But he was nice about it, he really was."

The McCarthys also insisted their son go to a school with an easily accessible Catholic church, preferably within walking distance of his dormitory room. So Dean Smith asked a local priest—and a heck of a Tar Heel fan—to write to the family. Another coach sent a picture of the nearby church, and threw in a box of candy, a tactic then considered strictly kosher.

Lefty Driesell, then the head coach at Davidson, called one day, and, as usual, Colonel McCarthy inquired about the church in Charlotte, North Carolina, a Baptist stronghold.

Driesell allowed as how he thought there might be a Catholic church seven miles, or so, outside town, but he wasn't really sure.

"That," says Colonel McCarthy, "settled that."

Driesell presumably has polished up his act considerably since those days. Mrs. Dantley admits her son probably would not have given Maryland even a second thought until the former encyclopedia salesman gave them his pitch.

"I find him so personable and easy to talk to," Mrs. Dantley said in March 1973. "When all this first started, Maryland wasn't even in it. Then I met Lefty. He turned me right around. He's the most dynamic. He spent the first 45 minutes talking about nothing but education, like he was interested in Adrian's coming just to be a student."

Bobby Knight, the Indiana coach, impressed Mrs. Dantley because he seemed to be the most serious.

Dean Smith told her if her son spent the same amount of time on his lessons in college as he spent in class during high school, he would have no problems. "I had never thought about that before," she said.

North Carolina State's Norm Sloan told Mrs. Dantley and Adrian that when he recruited David Thompson, State's sophomore All-America, he promised he'd have good players to go with him. "Now he's promising Adrian the same thing," said Mrs. Dantley. "He appealed to his ego."

Bill Musselman, the Minnesota coach, "doesn't smile all that much," said Mrs. Dantley. "When he does, you know he's sincere.

"I like talking to most of them, and then I go back and read things about them and hear things about them and I say, 'Can this be the same man who sat here on my couch, in my living room?'

"They all tell me that Adrian is the key to their winning next year. I know when he signs they'll probably win some and they'll probably lose some.

"When they're here, they all look so sincere. I'm always thinking, 'They need my boy, they need my boy.' But when they leave, I get a little more rational. They probably say the same thing to everybody."

Mrs. Dantley, who divorced Adrian's father when her son was three, shares her apartment with her sister, Mrs. Muriel Jenkins, and her son, Frankie Jenkins, who was 14 when Dantley was being recruited.

All of them have attended Adrian's games since his freshman season at De Matha, "and we are going to owe our lives to the company store next year," Mrs. Jenkins said. "We'll try and go to as many games as we can."

The sisters are extremely close, though not to the point of substantiating the rumor that "the aunt had all the influence on Adrian." "We heard that a couple of times," said Mrs. Dantley, "and it really tickled me."

At the Dapper Dan tournament, Jerry Tarkanian, the newly appointed head coach at Nevada–Las Vegas, thought Mrs. Jenkins was Mrs. Dantley. "We were having a nice conversation," Mrs. Jenkins recalled, grinning from ear to ear. "Then I told him who I was. He dropped me like a hot potato. 'Got to find Mrs. Dantley,' he mumbled, and turned around and left, looking for my sister."

Adrian scratched Marquette from his final choices for several reasons. He did not think Al McGuire would be at the Milwaukee school all four years, and worse, Hank Raymond, a Marquette assistant, called one day, and Mrs. Jenkins happened to pick up the phone. "He kept calling her hon and honey," Adrian recalled. "I didn't like it."

Dantley visited Florida in May 1973, simply because Terry Truax, the school's assistant coach, was a former De Matha assistant and a long-time friend of the family.

The weekend of the Dapper Dan, Truax just happened to be on the same flight out of Washington as the Dantley contingent. He rented a car at the Pittsburgh airport, took Mrs. Dantley, Mrs. Jenkins, and Frankie to one of the practice sites, and drove them back to the hotel, all perfectly legal since he was going their way, anyway.

Dean Smith also just happened to be on the plane when Adrian, his mother, his aunt, and his cousin flew back to Washington. Of course, he had a car waiting to drive them all home. Smith was dynamite at airports.

All of these "coincidences" occurred through most of her son's senior basketball year for Mrs. Dantley, as they do for most parents of other highly recruited athletes.

But the next year, there were no special favors. Mrs. Dantley no longer was asked to have lunch with a North Carolina Congressman, an N.C. State alumnus. Maryland Governor Marvin Mandel never called to ask Adrian and his mother to come over to the mansion in Annapolis, to take a boat ride down the Severn while Mandel put in a good word for his old pal, Lefty Driesell. Arnold Palmer didn't write, nor did Senator Hubert Humphrey's man offer to pop for a meal at the Senate dining room, or anywhere else.

"When a kid finally makes his choice, it can really be tough on the parents," says Georgetown coach John Thompson. "All of a sudden people don't stop to say hello, they don't call you, they don't knock on your door. They don't pay any attention to you at all. Some parents can't handle it. I've seen it happen so many times."

George Raveling, former Maryland assistant and now head coach at Washington State, says McMillen's mother often asked why he never called her any more after her son enrolled at College Park.

But Austin Carr's father had no such withdrawal problems. "It began to get like a circus, anyway, being invited to lunches and dinners and cocktail parties," he says. "The day Austin signed, and it went out over the national news wires, I was the most relieved man in the world, and so was my son.

"People left us alone. I remember Austin made his

decision before he was going to play in one of those all-star games in Allentown, Pennsylvania. We went there and the coaches were running after all those kids trying to get them to sign. But they left us alone. They knew Austin had signed and they just let him play ball. They all congratulated him, and they all congratulated me. It was really nice."

During Austin's freshman year his father busied himself by putting together several scrapbooks of his son's accomplishments, and went to every Notre Dame game he could afford, even if Austin only played in the freshman preliminary.

"I'm very proud of my son," Austin Carr, Sr., said, standing in the tastefully decorated living room of his new home in Northwest Washington, purchased in 1972 with part of the $1 million Austin, Jr., received as the Cavaliers' first-round draft pick. "It was hectic," he said, "but I guess you could say it was worth it." His dream had also come true.

8 / The Developer

FOR MOST HIGH SCHOOL COACHES, a player of Adrian Dantley's caliber comes along once in a lifetime. For Morgan Wootten, the 42-year-old coach at De Matha High School, it almost had been a yearly occurrence since he had arrived at the Hyattsville, Maryland, Catholic school in 1956.

He had coached a dozen high school All-America players and countless more All-Metropolitan stars before Dantley showed up, and he was justly proud of his placement record: Every De Matha senior basketball player the previous 13 years had been awarded a college scholarship.

Wootten's record was, and still is, unmatched on the high school level. Through the 1974 season his teams had won 492 games and lost 69, many of the defeats suffered against college freshman or junior varsity teams.

His teams were ranked No. 1 of all the Catholic schools

in America four times and were named the Washington area's No. 1 team for 12 of the last 14 seasons.

The entire 1965 De Matha basketball team was voted into the Basketball Hall of Fame after it inflicted the only defeat Power Memorial Academy of New York City suffered in the Lew Alcindor era. That game was played before more than 13,000 at Maryland's Cole Field House that year, and De Matha's victory ended Power's 71-game streak.

De Matha itself, an old brick building surrounded on all sides by parking lots, lies tucked away behind a new-car dealership a few blocks from the center of Hyattsville, a smallish, working-class suburb less than five miles from the District of Columbia line. The school has been in financial difficulties for years, though its tuition has always been reasonable. Dantley paid $650 per year, the same rate as every other student, basketball player or not.

Wootten had come to De Matha as a history teacher and basketball coach two years after graduating from the University of Maryland. He didn't play ball for the Terrapins, although he did have a rather undistinguished playing career at Montgomery County Junior College before entering Maryland.

He now has a lifetime contract with De Matha, whose current principal once served as Wootten's assistant coach. He has written two basketball handbooks, one a technical study of his "blitz defense," and he has been in constant demand on the basketball-clinic circuit over the last few years. Each summer, several hundred Washington area players also attend a summer camp he operates in partnership with Joe Gallagher, the basketball coach at St. John's High School. It often has been said that Wootten has turned down college jobs to avoid taking a pay cut. Even while Dantley was still at De Matha, he turned down one offer from an eastern school that would have provided a five-year contract at $45,000 per year.

Wootten lives a rather unpretentious life. He, his wife, Kathy, and their five children live in a quiet Washington suburb less than 15 minutes away from the school. His office in a corner of the minuscule De Matha gymnasium seems barely adequate. The paneling is faded, his desk is cluttered with papers, and his windowsill is piled high with boxes containing letters from college coaches eager to acquire the services of his players. On one wall hangs a framed replica of John Wooden's cliché-cluttered credo, "The Pyramid of Success."

Wootten stands about 5-foot-10, and wears his hair fairly short and his sideburns straight and clipped just above the ears. He has developed a slight paunch in recent years. He likes to drink beer at home and at cocktail parties. At De Matha, he constantly sips tea prepared on a hotplate.

Wootten's teams have been known for their calm, reasoned approach to the game. The coach himself is a stickler for detail and drill. He has won with big men and small men, whites and blacks. And he, too, recruits. He has all manner of contacts on the playgrounds of Washington. His friends recommend players to him. He scouts the summer leagues, the CYO leagues, the Boys' Club leagues, the inner-city junior high school leagues. And, of course, his summer camp attracts many of the area's finest prospects.

"Every black kid in Washington dreams about playing at De Matha," says Michael Morton, a player Wootten spotted in a church league in the eighth grade. He was 6-5 then and has grown three inches since. Last season, he was De Matha's starting center. A year later, though, his dreams had changed. Morton transferred to Eastern High.

Dantley himself showed up at the school unannounced,

because his friend, James Brown, a former high school All-America, had recommended the place.

Though Wootten does not particularly care to make the comparison, Dantley may be the most talented player he has ever coached. He became a starter in his third game with the varsity while still a freshman, and no one had ever done that before.

Some of Wootten's other talented players have been Johnny Jones (Los Angeles State and the Boston Celtics), Joe Kennedy (Duke and the now-defunct Pittsburgh Condors), Sid Catlett (Notre Dame and the Cleveland Cavaliers), John Austin (Boston College and the Baltimore Bullets), Bernie Williams (LaSalle and the Virginia Squires), and James Brown (Harvard). Many more are still playing major-college basketball.

Dantley, though, was probably among the more protected of Wootten's wonders. The coach was well aware of the amount of pressure the recruiters could bring to bear against impressionable teen-agers. Even as Dantley entered ninth grade, still fresh on the coach's mind was an incident the year before when James Brown collapsed during a game and was hospitalized for nervous exhaustion.

Wootten said in an interview on May 2, 1973, five weeks before Dantley would make his final decision, "There are eight schools still in the running for Adrian. If Adrian would give as much time to the coaches of those schools as they each wanted, he could spend 45 hours a week being recruited. My job is to avoid that."

Dantley's parents had been divorced when he was three. Wootten simply became the most dominant male in his life during his four years of high school, and the boy's mother appreciated it. "I don't know what we would have done without Morgan," she says, often. "He knew exactly what to do in every situation. I love the man, I really do."

So strong was the attachment between family and coach that Dantley once admitted he probably would have followed Wootten to Maryland if he had accepted a job offer there as assistant coach in April 1973. "It would have made the decision a lot easier," he said.

And that was one of the reasons Wootten turned down Lefty Driesell's offer. According to several of his friends, he did not want people to think the coaching job was part of a package deal, incumbent upon Dantley's attending the university.

There have been other kinds of offers, too. "Some coaches leave things on the borderline edge so that if you make a push, you could make yourself a nice fistful of money by sending them a kid," Wootten said.

"We're in a situation where people know you can't buy De Matha players. And word has gotten out that you can't buy the coaching staff. But I know for a fact that people have told Adrian he'll be the best-dressed kid on campus if he goes to their school. A lot of junior colleges tell you the community will take care of the kid's needs.

"I would hope that our kids would know better. One of our players this year told me one school offered to supply him with stereo equipment, the whole bit. [The player was Billy Langloh; the school, a Southern Conference power.] But he turned it off right away, and, of course, the school was eliminated."

Once a coach has crossed Wootten, has violated his strict rule that all correspondence and contact between a college and a De Matha player come through him, he would be wasting his time and breath attempting to recruit at the school any further.

George King, when he was the basketball coach at West Virginia (he's now athletic director at Purdue), found that out. It began with a phone call. In 1966 King was courting

De Matha's Bob Whitmore and his teammate Bernie Williams, now with the Virginia Squires. He would treat them both to dinner, then return them home at a decent hour, he told Wootten.

"Whitmore was just getting over the flu," Wootten recalled, "so I agreed to let King take Bernie." But King wound up at Whitmore's apartment anyway, and enticed the youngster out of his sickbed and into a restaurant. Williams caught Whitmore's bug that night, and an impending game against the American University freshmen had to be rescheduled later in the season, two days before De Matha was to play the Maryland freshman team, a powerful foe.

"Well, we beat American, had only one day to prepare for Maryland, and lost by a point," Wootten said. "It was our only defeat that year."

A few months later, King, who had since been named basketball coach at Purdue, called and asked permission to speak to Whitmore, literally pleading forgiveness for the earlier incident, Wootten said. The call came the day before Whitmore was to announce his enrollment at Notre Dame at a lavish press conference. King was so informed.

"The next day," Wootten said, still bristling over the memory seven years later, "Bob tells me George King called him at midnight to try and talk him out of it. Stayed on the phone almost an hour. I don't think I've spoken to George King since."

While Dantley was agonizing about choosing a college, Wootten tried not to influence his decision in any way, though he warned the Minnesota coach that unless a pesky assistant stopped visiting Dantley at home, unannounced, the school would be dropped from consideration.

"We had an alumnus of a Southeastern Conference school call and I told him our guidelines," Wootten said.

"He said he *thought* his coach would follow them. I just said, 'If he doesn't, you're out of it.'

"The high school coach really has to be on his toes, but he can't make the decision for the kid. I've always said I don't tell them where to go to school, just like I don't tell them who to marry."

Roy Henderson, Bruce Buckley's coach at nearby Bladensburg High, tried the same approach with his young high school All-America, but he confessed in March of Buckley's senior year, "I'd kind of like Bruce to play for Dean Smith. They play smart basketball at North Carolina, they work together. There's not a lot of brute force, or one-on-one play. It's pure, intelligent ball. An unselfish, talented player like Bruce can do well for them."

Buckley was the first legitimate blue-chip prospect Henderson, then 36, had ever coached in his 10 years at the suburban public high school. He had been an assistant when Bruce's brother Jay, the school's first high school All-America, was a senior, "but I was never really involved in it that much," he said.

Henderson admitted, quite frankly, that he was awed at times as representatives of America's most prestigious colleges and universities knocked on the door to his tiny office and asked to come in. Occasionally he even found himself grilling them, as they sat on his battered couch, to explain a zone press here, a weakside play there.

Though his coaching record was a gaudy 155-45, Henderson had never written a book or a pamphlet. He usually paid to attend clinics, unlike his counterpart at De Matha, who was paid to speak at them.

Henderson had played college basketball at Washington College in Chestertown, Maryland, but he was a better baseball pitcher, and spent a year in a Nebraska rookie league in the Washington Senators' farm system. He coached at Bladensburg Junior High for three years, assisting the high school's varsity coach, and coached basketball at nearby Central High for two years before going back to Bladensburg in 1963, for good.

Before Buckley, the closest Henderson came to handling a blue-chipper occurred in 1970, when Danny Elliot, a 6-foot guard, averaged 30 points a game, led the Washington area in scoring, and was named to the prestigious All-Metropolitan team. Elliot went on to Virginia Tech, but Howie Shannon, the coach who had recruited him, resigned after his freshman season, and Elliot was unable to get along with the man who replaced him, volatile Don DeVoe. "They told him he was too slow," Henderson said, "and it really hurt me. There is no way that boy could not have played for that team."

But Elliot failed out of school and came back home. He worked for a while as an auto-parts salesman, went back to a local junior college, and never played basketball at a four-year school.

While most colleges came to Wootten literally pleading for his players, Henderson found himself trying to convince coaches to take a chance on his boys. Bladensburg drew many of its students from poor, predominantly black sections of town, and many of his players had eligibility problems. "They don't understand that just because you can play ball, a school will not come chasing you," Henderson said. "They don't believe it until it's too late. Some of them go to junior colleges, but they don't usually stay. It bothers me, it really does. I don't want that to happen with Bruce."

After Buckley's sophomore year, Henderson met with the youngster and his mother to discuss how they would handle the horde of coaches who would be descending on the school and their home. "Roy has been running interference," Mildred Buckley said. "The ones that come here [to her home] come by invitation really, people I want to talk to and people that want to talk with Bruce a little more."

Henderson handled most of the contact between Buckley and the interested schools. He arranged to give Buckley a free period in the afternoon to talk with recruiters, and he did not give out the Buckleys' unlisted home telephone number unless Bruce or his mother showed interest in the school.

"Everyone was cooperative, we had no trouble at all," said Henderson. "Duke put the most pressure on him: 'When are you going to visit? When are you going to decide?'—that sort of thing."

Duke coach Bucky Waters, in fact, had recruited Jay Buckley to the Durham school when he was Vic Bubas' assistant. During Bruce's sophomore and junior years, Waters was the only coach in America to have the Buckleys' home telephone number.

Still, Buckley finally scorned Waters for Dean Smith and North Carolina, the school that had put him under no pressure or duress. Henderson, of course, was delighted. "They're an amazing group of people," he said. "They never tried to sell Bruce. They were friendly without being Mr. Personality, Mr. Efficiency. A lot of coaches come on too strong. They seemed like ordinary good guys. They just said, 'We'd like to have you,' and that was that."

The entire North Carolina coaching staff managed to visit Buckley's home the summer and fall of his senior year, and he was offered a scholarship before his final basketball season had even started. Mrs. Buckley was concerned about that. "She thought it might be a good idea to keep a small school in mind just in case Bruce had a bad year or was injured," Henderson said. "John Lotz [a Carolina assistant, now head coach at Florida] told her that wasn't necessary.

Bruce had a scholarship there no matter what. She was very impressed.

"This was Bruce's decision to make, and with a kid like Bruce, who knows what he wants, I just tried to keep his life as normal as possible. Really, I didn't feel any extra pressure on myself. I actually enjoyed it. No one harassed me or bothered me. Oh, maybe a few more phone calls than usual.

"But basically, it was a pretty normal year."

9 / The Middlemen

THE EYES of a dozen coaches snapped to attention. To their astonishment, there was the mother of Adrian Dantley chatting casually with the most famous middleman of them all, Freddie the Spook.

The chat, at the Dapper Dan tournament, was all very innocent. Virginia Dantley was in the company of wiser friends at the time and did not learn until later the magnitude of the man who introduced himself as Fred Stegman and soon began writing the names of colleges on a handy napkin.

She had been more amused than alarmed by the experience and wondered—as did others—how this slippery looking man with the stringy hair and inexpensive suit could possibly strike so much fear in so many hearts.

But like his cigar, Stegman's reputation burns steadily. It is whispered that Stegman was given $7,000 one year by a college in North Carolina and never delivered a player; that the mere mention of his name in connection with a school is enough to bring NCAA probation.

Stegman insists he is overrated by his critics. He freely admits he used to think there was money to be made acting as a middleman between prospects and coaches, but he claims to have made "only $3,000 in my best year." If he is selling players at the rates some believe, he hides it well.

"When I was 15," says Marquette coach Al McGuire, "he strayed over to Rockaway Beach, where we lived. He came into the house for a drink of water once and stayed three days."

In *Foul*, the biography of Connie Hawkins, author David Wolf describes the Spook as "a thin black man in his early forties, a cigar dangling in the corner of his mouth," who "prowls the [New York] schoolyards, community centers and high school gyms, lining up players for whatever college will pay him the most."

Stegman quarrels with one point. He is white. The nickname (he detests it) was bestowed some 20 years ago by Al McGuire's brother, Dick, because of Stegman's ghostlike ability to be wherever he thought he ought to be to protect an investment. His territory remains the back roads and back rooms, although he has given up his habit of carrying his merchandise lists inside his coat—one pocket containing a list of his available guards, another his forwards, and still another his pivot men.

"Need any Jucos?" he frequently asks coaches, referring to his specialty, junior-college players. Lately he has branched out into representing college players, in their negotiations with the pros.

Long-time acquaintances insist Stegman did away with his tramplike qualities when he married several years ago, having met his wife, Clare, in Mount Airy, North Carolina, en route to recruit Artis Gilmore. All admire his flair for grandly ordering drinks for himself and his companions, then deftly drifting to another group when the check arrives.

"Most of the coaches—I call 'em the $300 suits—don't want to be seen with me in public," he admits. "But they'll get to me behind closed doors, or over the phone. When your program's hurting, I come out of the woodwork. I'm the front man for the $300 suits."

The McGuires are among the few who admit to a friendship with Stegman, who provided Al McGuire his first players in McGuire's first college head-coaching job—Belmont Abbey.

"I sent him four kids," Stegman says. "One of 'em I took out of a crap game in the schoolyards after he flunked his entrance exam to Iona College." Both McGuire and Stegman insist that was an act of friendship. Stegman maintains there have been all too many similar deals with less reputable coaches.

"I thought it would be—what do you say?—a great cup of tea, that I could make $6,000 or so a year. It never amounted to anything, let me tell you. The kids try to use you and the coaches are even worse. Some of these men have slept in my house so they could save $15 a night for a hotel room and slip the money to the kid."

Stegman claims to have "placed" about 200 players in "60 to 70" schools as a "scout" over the years and been involved in only one NCAA probation, Wichita State.

In his time, Stegman claims to have found Lenny Wilkens for Providence College. He says he has been indirectly responsible for breaking the basketball color line at the University of Tennessee and providing scholarship aid for dozens of players unable to advance beyond the playgrounds without someone with contacts. He is the only middleman who gives references.

One of his references, Jack Bruen, an assistant coach at De Matha and one of Dantley's escorts for his Dapper Dan trip, says he probably would not have gone to college had it not been for Stegman. Bruen says the University of Scranton offered him a scholarship, then withdrew it after most of the other schools had filled their quotas.

"Freddie just happened by school [Power Memorial], heard about it, and gave me a name and number to call," says Bruen. The number was for Catholic University; the name, former coach Bill Gardner. Bruen was offered a four-year scholarship, sight unseen, and he earned his degree.

"We were gonna bring Artis Gilmore and Ernie Fleming and Kenny Durrett and Petie Gibson in for a visit when Gardner-Webb was a two-year school," Stegman recalls, "only we suddenly realized there's no blacks at the school. So we go around town and the ones nearby and bring some in to sit around the dinner hall and whatever." Gilmore and Fleming attended Gardner-Webb; Durrett and Gibson went elsewhere. All the prospects were treated royally, though, by the Gardner-Webb angel, a lay preacher who ran a trucking firm.

"He'd stand and give a sort of sermon to each group of kids who visited," Stegman says. " 'Do not sin, do not steal,' he'd say. Then each kid would find a $5 bill under the knife and fork."

Gilmore, who later signed a $1 million contract with the American Basketball Association after leading Jacksonville to the NCAA finals, confirms both Gardner-Webb stories.

"I remember it like it was yesterday," he says. "But I don't want to drag up old wounds, so to speak. The man is dead now anyway."

There are Stegman-like operators in each major city, each trying to land that one gifted player who could set him up for years. Stegman thought his might be Lew Alcindor from Power Memorial [High] in New York City.

"I was over there every day, with the coach and the brothers," he says. "But I never got to talk to the kid. Now what would Alcindor be worth to me—$10,000 a year maybe?"

A former All-Metropolitan explained how a Washington, D.C., middleman, Nevil Waters, operated. "Many of the recruiters would set up dinners and appointments through him," the former player said. "He'd get us together, and lots of times go with us to dinner or on trips. Just to get a kid interested, talking to a school, had to be worth something. He'd call and say, 'Don't plan anything Monday because so-and-so is coming to town, and I've got this guy set up with you for the weekend.' I'd cancel whatever I had planned."

Waters was a fifth-grade teacher at Simmons Elementary who spoke proudly of his "advanced degrees in guidance and counseling from George Washington University."

"You name a coach and I probably know him," Waters said. "All I try and do is help a young kid get into schools. Mostly it's kids going to city high schools, the ones that don't get the exposure some of the others might. I have a lot of contacts. I used to play a lot of ball. Dean Smith and me played in an AAU league when we both were in the service. Bucky Waters is a good friend; so is the fellow at Syracuse.

"These guys will call me up and ask, 'Who's good?' and I'll tell 'em. I just get satisfaction from doing it. It's my life. Nobody ever paid me, though. Yeah, I heard this stuff about me being a flesh peddler and all that. Just tell 'em to send me the cash, cause I've never seen any of it."

Stegman claims to be doing his biggest business as a pro agent lately. His state of "semiretirement" hardly is voluntary. Ironically, Stegman achieved his fame for the alleged ability to deliver black players; now he is being eased out by black flesh peddlers.

"His days are over," says George Raveling, who helped recruit Maryland to prominence before becoming head coach at Washington State. "Recruiting is too sophisticated now. There aren't any sleepers. It used to be I could go down south and grab a kid nobody knew about. In Alabama 10 years ago they were shooting blacks who tried to get into school. Now they start four."

The black man who has made the most rapid rise in the behind-the-scenes aspects of recruiting in recent years, the one with a bundle of impressive players from talent-thick New York City is Rodney Parker, who also has a reputation for being able to produce tickets to nearly every event in Madison Square Garden.

Parker began attracting national attention in the early '70s as the man who helped tame Fly, an extremely gifted player whose background included fights and sit-downs, broken chairs and a broken bone or two even before he outscored most of the collegiate players in the country for two years at Austin Peay State College in Tennessee.

Fly is called James Williams by the few who neither know nor appreciate the magnitude of his escapades and talents. Each of his intimates, from the mother who held little hope of his advancing much beyond the 500 block of Stone Avenue in Brooklyn, to Parker to the assistant headmaster of a prep school—has a favorite Fly tale. Fly admits most are true, and also that "I wouldn't want anyone following in my footsteps."

Fly began dribbling a basketball and tossing it into the most convenient round receptacle—a garbage can—at age six. In his high school years, although he rarely attended Madison High, his tantrums overshadowed his considerable skills on the court. There was a memorable gesture toward the Boys' High crowd during a playoff and other fits of temper. When Fly felt thirsty after scoring a layup, his teammates rushed to play defense while Fly rushed to the nearest fountain.

Fly would go to school, but not often to class, preferring "to hang around with the women all the time. All the time, you know?" His sisters would finish his homework while Fly, who acquired the nickname after an especially awkward-looking shot, polished his moves against neighborhood competition that included Phil Sellers, later a star at Rutgers, and Ron Haigler, later of Penn.

The accepted rule in New York—and perhaps in most other metropolitan areas—is that only about 20 per cent of the excellent playground players advance beyond the playground, and it was assumed that Fly would be a part of the vast majority for once in his life.

But Parker started pushing Fly, and a number of other players, out of the ghetto and toward a prep school in upstate New York called Glen Springs Academy that specializes in "chronic underachievers." Fly once was coaxed into saying 300 colleges had recruited him, but Parker claims that was an exaggeration, by about 285.

"Listen, the word was out on him—bad attitude, impossible to handle," Parker says. "Face it, he'd been in and out of more schools than he could score points."

At Glen Springs, with his family providing the required $100 per month in fees, Fly attended classes regularly. Surprisingly, he began enjoying it, although he was far from a scholar and still had trouble controlling his temper. Against Elmira Free Academy, Fly grabbed a chair and swung it during an on-the-court fight. Self-defense, he later claimed—there were four players after him. Another time the opposition tried a slowdown against Glen Springs and

Fly sat himself right down on the court and refused to budge.

One day Fly, Craig Jackson, and another black player went into a snack bar in downtown Watkins Glen and were refused service. "A year before I'd have ripped that place apart," he said later, "just for something to do as much as anything. But the three of us just walked out of there silently."

Fly seriously considered only Murray State and Austin Peay "because he wanted to go where he could be seen," his mother says. He chose Austin Peay primarily because of an assistant named Leonard Hamilton, an exceptional pitchman Fly and Parker sometimes introduced as "Cousin Al" to keep other recruiters from pestering him.

At a recent junior-college tournament, Stegman surveyed an atmosphere he had seen a hundred other times in dozens of other small towns: predominantly black teams playing to predominantly white audiences, cheerleaders either in tears or ecstasy, and intense coaches trying to escape to a better life.

"To me this is small-time recruiting," he said. "Until you see the Dean Smiths and Leftys and Frank McGuires, it's nothing."

Unimpressed, he headed for a lounge reserved for officials and coaches, demonstrating along the way the glib, city-slicker style often effective in the innocent, teetotaling hinterlands.

Inside, Stegman discovered a coach who had introduced himself in a diner earlier in the day and requested his phone number, just in case he happened to be in New York sometime. The coach nudged a major-college assistant and pointed to Stegman. "Fred's gonna send me a good one," he said.

Later, Big-Time Assistant made it a point to catch Stegman during a lull in the action. "Listen, Fred, I'm not one to go beating around the bush," he said. "Tell me, how much would it cost me to come up to New York and get me a center?"

Stegman was clearly caught off-guard by such a direct approach and the reply stumbled from his mouth, like a double dribble. "Well, ah, I don't really have a fixed price."

"If I came up, would you show me around?" Big-Time Assistant said.

"Be glad to, my man," Stegman said, recovering nicely.

When the games were completed and the receipts were being totaled, the fate of a Pittsburgh, Pennsylvania, linebacker was being decided in a narrow corridor.

"Listen, I got me a linebacker," said a middleman called Boxcar. "He's a sleeper. He's not from a good high school, but he can play."

"Has he got a price on his head?" said the junior-college football coach.

"Oh, a quarter, 50 cents [$250 or $500]," said Boxcar. "Now he quit once. It was a bad situation, racial trouble just about every day."

"He quit once, he might quit here," the coach reflected.

"If he does, you know what to do," said Boxcar. "Get rid of him."

"See me in the office tomorrow," the coach said.

Those who consider college athletic recruiting less than morally correct consider middlemen almost repulsive. John Thompson, Georgetown University basketball coach, recalls an ugly feeling in his stomach after learning that a close friend and counselor for years figured to receive $5,000 had he gone to Cincinnati and not Providence.

"One guy I'll never forget," the 6-11 Thompson says,

"was one of those middlemen coming in and telling me, 'The tree is fruitful, make sure you harvest right.' Somehow, he thought I was going to Notre Dame, so he said: 'Notre Dame's good, but you can't eat it.'

"He didn't care where I went. He just wanted to represent me. He said, 'Let me talk for you.' That happens today, and a lot of high school coaches back off it and make believe they don't hear and see it, because if the deal comes down on them they can say, 'I didn't know. I thought this guy was some kind of guidance counselor or adviser.'

"They [the recruiters] are in a household where the parents are elated over all this newfound publicity and out it starts . . . Austin Carr . . . a million dollars . . . fur coats . . . big house . . . my son, I see him . . . even though they [the recruiters] know for a fact that being a superstar is a one-in-a-million shot."

Still, there are some redeeming traits for some middlemen, some claim.

"Like when an assistant coach gets off a plane in New York, or any other large city, he could waste two hours just trying to find the high school," says Al McGuire, a practical man. "Guys like Freddie cut down time considerably. They take you where the action is. Fred knows more people at the high school and college level than anyone I know. He knows his basketball."

Stegman is annoyed that his former colleague, Howie Garfinkel, has profited handsomely lately. From his New York apartment, Garfinkel produces scouting reports on high school players that are thorough, accurate, and amusing and sell for $150 per season.

The NCAA even sanctions Garfinkel and his less respected competitors. All of which infuriates Stegman. "Tell me, I send you two players and what do you give me?" Stegman said to a junior-college coach.

"Nothing," the coach said.

"I give you two players and you don't give me a cent," Stegman said. "But you pay Garfinkel $125 a season [his price has increased since the conversation] and he don't give you nothing."

In fact, Garfinkel's service is considered a bargain by most college coaches, because his single-spaced data includes the name of the prospect, his high school and coach, height, weight, race, and—most important—class standing, grade average, College Board scores, and an evaluation of ability.

From October through June, Garfinkel offers preseason and progress reports on about 1,000 seniors he feels have the potential to play at some collegiate level, from small college to what he calls "the big time." For schools with modest recruiting budgets, the $150-per-year fee is much less than what it would cost a coach to gather the information, and the service provides the two most significant factors in judging a prospect—whether he can get into a school and whether he can play at its level.

"I write 'em up and let the chips fall where they may," says Garfinkel, who has been offering his reports since the mid-'60s. "I saw a kid over in Brooklyn once who looked great but didn't know what a scholarship was. I wrote him up, that unless I'd seen a mirage he was a real sleeper. In three weeks the kid got 50 letters and a lot of phone calls. I write that a kid's a disaster and he still gets 10 offers. I double the exposure for every kid in the country."

For basketball players along the East Coast and in the Midwest, a positive report by Garfinkel is an almost certain sign that the phone will begin jangling shortly and that the postman also will ring . . . and ring . . . and ring. Garfinkel rates his players on a system of one ("average to mediocre") to five ("great or potentially great"). He rated

Adrian Dantley "an eight, one of the three or four best high school players I've ever seen."

Garfinkel's reports are read for their entertainment as well as their informational value. Some of his better one-line descriptions:

"Thinking man's backcourter."

"Carries you to the final four."

"Shoots the postage-stamp jumper to 17 feet."

"More moves than Flipper in deep [of Dantley]."

"Talks with God three times a quarter."

"Blue-chip talent and if he gets it off his shoulder will be outstanding collegian."

"Too nice a kid to knock but if Leo Durocher was right this loosey-goosey, happy-go-lucky cornerman with pro strength and physique is not prime-time candidate for high majors."

"Skills are limited. Has an uncle 6-11. Big Timers recruit the uncle."

"Comes at you like the White Tornado & obliterates all who stand in path regardless of score."

"Mostly, I bat 80 per cent," Garfinkel says. "I'm 95, maybe 99 per cent accurate on grades" (often he gets them from the prospect or his high school). As a judge of talent, he is much better than he was as a player. "I'm 5-11, 165, and can't go to my left," he admits. "In high school I was the seventh man on the worst basketball team in New York. I would have been a one, maybe a half, not recruitable. I wouldn't have made my own report."

To those who claim that Stegman—and others—pushed players unqualified academically to college (and he admits he has), his reply is that the coach and admissions officer always could have said no.

"The thing about Fred is that he's basically honest," John Thompson said during the Dapper Dan tournament, sweeping his hand about a crowded hotel lobby. "You know what he is. Some of these other guys do the same thing, only they come off as respectable."

Stegman's major worry is his next pitch, his next long bus trip to Nowhere. "Here he is, the world-famous flesh peddler," he once said of himself in a barker's tones. "He has a cast on his hand [from a recent fall] and glasses because some punks beat him up three years ago. He looks like this and people claim he's makin' a bundle off every kid in the country."

Stegman laughed. "Next time, my boy, I ain't taking . . . what you call it? . . . no pile of hay. Next time I want the farm."

10 / The Alumni: Help or Hindrance?

THE YEAR WAS 1968, and Lefty Driesell was making a heavy pitch to acquire the services of De Matha All-America James Brown for his first Maryland team. Unfortunately for him, so was Harvard. The former encyclopedia salesman simply was outclassed.

Harvard asked one of its more persuasive alumni for help, and Senator Edward Kennedy was more than willing to oblige. One day he took Brown and his coach, Morgan Wootten, to lunch in the Senate dining room. A few weeks later they all had dinner together.

Brown eventually signed with Harvard, and though Driesell now insists "the Kennedy thing really wasn't that important to me," he obviously thought otherwise.

He wrote the senator a letter— "Aw, it wasn't nothing but a joke, really," Driesell said later—asking Kennedy for his help in recruiting athletes to Maryland. "I just told him he'd probably have a better chance seeing a kid play here than he would at Harvard," said the coach, who was not smiling.

Kennedy wrote back to say that he hoped someday to help the coach recruit a Massachusetts boy—as long as Harvard wasn't interested in him. Driesell has never taken him up on the offer, however, and the letter is tacked to a bulletin board in an assistant coach's office, buried under a pile of papers.

"I don't base my recruiting program on other people helping me," insisted Driesell, who nevertheless had few qualms about asking Maryland Governor Marvin Mandel to invite Adrian Dantley and his mother over to the mansion for dinner.

It was not such an unusual request. All over America, legitimate and "synthetic" alumni—people who did not attend a certain school but contribute time and money to the athletic program—actively proselytize. Most are content to give to a scholarship fund; others prefer a more active role.

At Arkansas, several members of the Razorback Club, the school's alumni association, own airplanes which are conveniently available to football coach Frank Broyles at all times. In the Southwest Conference, as one coach said, "if you don't fly, you die" in the recruiting wars.

At one Big Ten school, an alumnus who is a rabid hockey fan gives players a tremendous discount on their monthly rents in the apartment buildings he owns on campus. The school pays the players the normal $1,500 it would cost to live in the dorms, while their apartments cost less than $750 for the school year. The players simply pocket the difference.

In 1964, UCLA's basketball team had no starter taller than 6-foot-5. Yet the Bruins, who won a national championship that year, averaged eight more rebounds a game than their rivals. Of course they had a bit of incentive, according to Los Angeles *Times* writers Jeff Prugh and Dwight Chapin, authors of *The Wizard of Westwood,* a study of UCLA basketball and coach John Wooden.

Alumni put money for rebounds on a sliding scale. A player was paid $5 for each rebound up to 10 and $10 for each rebound beyond 10. "It was a helluva great feeling," says Jack Hirsch, a 6-3 forward on that team, "to pick up $100 bucks for a night's work. Believe me, we really went all out for rebounds." According to Keith Erickson of the Phoenix Suns, a forward for UCLA that year, Wooden knew nothing about the fund. "When he found out," says Erickson, "he stopped it."

At Kentucky, alumni frequently escort recruits to the Keeneland race track in Lexington, and if a boy should have extraordinary luck at the $2 window, so much the better. Apparently, many boys do.

"Let's just say a lot of people like to have a winning ticket," says a former chairman of the "Committee of 101," the booster group for Kentucky's basketball team.

The committee, now numbering close to 300 members, was formed in 1965 after a group of 101 fans sent a telegram to the team wishing them well on a road trip. Most committee members never attended college, let alone Kentucky, and only a handful own season tickets. The rest serve as ushers, vendors, and ticket takers, just to get on the inside.

"I never even went to college," says the benefactor, who works in Lexington's IBM plant. "I just love basketball, and Kentucky is the basketball capital of the world. It's the best way to be part of something. We're just people who love basketball, and we'll do anything to help the coaches ask."

One of the committee's favorite tactics is the airport reception. In 1973, when Kent Benson, a 6-11 prospect from New Castle, Indiana, stepped off a plane for a campus visit, 2,000 people were on hand to greet him, to touch him, to ask him for an autograph.

"It was a beautiful sight," the booster gushes. "We had people carrying signs, we had pictures of his face blown up into posters. The airport manager has a red carpet we roll out when a boy comes to town. And all the while, everybody was screaming 'We want you!' I don't know if he was embarrassed. He just kind of grinned and said he couldn't believe it. It lasted about 10 minutes, I guess, then everyone went home."

Benson eventually signed a grant-in-aid to attend Indiana.

The Committee of 101 also made other contributions. They paid for the installation of wall-to-wall carpeting in the Wildcat locker room and put in a stereo system, soft couches and chairs, and a color television in the training room.

"Anything we can do to make our players feel like they're at home, we'll do," the booster says. "We might take them out to dinner or to our homes. We've had members buy clothes for them. In recruiting, we'll go to a boy's high school game and talk to him and his parents. When that kid comes to town to visit, we try and show him a good time."

More than occasionally, alumni boosters go overboard. The former chairman of the Committee of 101 casually talks about providing Kentucky players with clothes. That is against the NCAA rules. So, too, is it illegal to talk to a prospect "at the site of his school's athletic competition," the NCAA has decreed.

According to the NCAA rule book, "If an institution's staff member requests an alumnus or other friend of the institution to recruit a particular prospect, then said alumnus becomes a representative of athletic interests of that institution." Translation: An alumnus must abide by all the rules and restrictions pertaining to his school's coaching staff.

Donald Dailey of Vienna, Virginia, is considered a representative of athletic interests in the Washington, D.C., area for the University of Washington. He scouts basketball talent for his alma mater "just as a hobby. I don't get a cent, not even for stamps."

Every school in America has its Donald Daileys, loyal graduates still proud of their old school ties and more than eager to push highly touted athletes in their areas toward their respective schools.

Dailey works harder than most. He is 37, a computer analyst for the CIA and a former reserve on the Washington basketball team. He has seen more than 200 high school basketball games since he began his scouting for the Huskies. He is a meticulous worker, and sends detailed scouting reports on D.C. area players before, during, and after each season. Five years ago Dailey wrote the following report on a pudgy, 6-3 De Matha High School freshman named Adrian Dantley:

"Sensational, unbelievable, out of this world. . . . If he doesn't make All-Metro, then he will definitely make it in the next three years. . . . He was born without nerves, cool under pressure. . . . I predict that Adrian will be a high school All-America in his senior year." Dailey was wrong on only one count. Dantley was an All-America in his junior year.

Still, though Washington had more than enough notice on Dantley, the school waited until March of his senior year before Dailey was given the go-ahead to arrange a campus visit to the Seattle school, 2,500 miles away.

By then, of course, Dantley had narrowed his choice to some eight schools, and the offer was politely refused, as

Dailey fully expected. He did, however, convince Larry Wright, a brilliant guard from Washington's Western High, to visit the campus. The day Wright was scheduled to leave, Washington's basketball coach, athletic director, and vice president in charge of minority affairs all flew in from the Coast to make sure the trip started off properly.

Wright spurned Washington—"It was just too far away," he says—for Grambling, located just five miles from the Louisiana town in which he had been born and raised before coming to Washington. "But at least we got him to go out and look," says Dailey. "It was a major breakthrough."

Though Dailey had been touting his old school for years to Washington-area talent, the coaching staff only recently sent him an NCAA rule book, detailing his role in the recruiting process.

"Before that, I did everything on instinct," he says. "Up until last year I never really did any recruiting. I prefer not to. Even now, I didn't talk to one kid until after the basketball season was over. I go through the coaches. That seemed like the right way to go about it."

Nevertheless, ignorance of the rules is no defense when an alumnus or other "representative" gets his school in trouble. NCAA files are loaded with cases in which these so-called representatives were among the primary reasons for schools being reprimanded, or placed on probation.

At Long Beach State, the NCAA charged, "a representative of the university's athletic interests cosigned a promissory note for a student-athlete and subsequently repaid the lending agency for the amount of the loan and . . . a representative . . . paid money to a lending agency to retire the balance of a loan originally obtained by a student-athlete at the time he was a prospect."

At Cornell "a representative of the university's athletic interests arranged for and paid the resultant costs of round-trip, commercial-airline transportation between Toronto, Canada, and Boston in order that two prospective athletes could be entertained. . . ."

At Oklahoma "a representative of the university's athletic interests transported the parents and friends of a student-athlete in a company-owned aircraft to attend a football game in Norman."

At North Carolina State "a representative of the university's athletic interests transported a prospective student athlete between his home and the institution's campus, and was reimbursed by the university for the cost of this transportation."

For almost every school placed on probation in the last five years, a "representative of athletic interests," translated alumnus, was cited by the NCAA in its published accounts of a member institution's transgressions.

But many alumni transgressions go largely undetected, simply because no records of illegal payments are kept.

Last summer a Big Ten football player detailed "how they took care of us." He requested anonymity because he still had a year of eligibility remaining, and he feared repercussions, and possible banishment from the team, if his name was made public.

"When I was being recruited, the assistant coaches made it pretty obvious what they could do for us," he said. "When I was on my visit to the campus, I was introduced to some people who said any time I needed anything, just call. A couple of 'em gave me their phone numbers."

As a freshman, the player was told to eat at a certain Pancake House on campus any time he felt like it. A friendly clothing merchant was pointed out, "and we could get up to $30 in clothes every time we went in." Every athlete also received passes for two to every movie house in the area.

All of that stopped the next season, the athlete said, when a new athletic director was appointed. "He told us he'd bust us if we broke the rules and he found out about it," the player said. "But mostly, we got the impression that he just didn't want to know."

The player still had no difficulty obtaining almost anything he desired. The procedure, he said, was ridiculously simple.

"You'd just go up to one of the assistant coaches and tell 'em you needed something. Then you'd go home and wait for them to call you. They'd give you a number and you'd call. It was always a pretty rich guy.

"Sometimes they'd ask you over to their house for dinner. One time a guy asked me to come over and shoot baskets with his kids in the backyard. Some guys just want your autograph. Then you'd go home, and a couple days later a letter would come with the cash you needed."

Once, in his sophomore year, the player needed $500 for a down payment on a car. "It was the same thing. I had this guy's number and I'd call. He took me out to dinner, nice steak, everything, and then he drove me back to my apartment. He handed me the envelope and that was it.

"I don't like to ask for money, and I don't unless I'm really in a bind. I've got my pride, too. But I look at it like this. I'm here because I play football. I work hard at it, I've been hurt real bad, and during the season it's a full-time job. Why shouldn't I get paid something extra?"

"It's up to us to inform our people what they can and what they cannot do," says Maryland athletic director Jim Kehoe, who claims he reads the NCAA rule book every night. "The institution is responsible for all these people's actions. But how in hell can you control, monitor, and supervise them all? In all our newsletters to alumni, we tell them 'Don't get involved yourself, work through the coaching staff.' But that doesn't really prevent you from stubbing your toe.

"We had a fellow up in Maine, an alumnus of the school, and he watched a high school basketball game. After the game he goes down and shakes hands with this kid and tells him he's from the University of Maryland. That's a violation. You can't contact a student-athlete at the site of a competition. These are well-intentioned, generous people, so how do you control them? How do I know if somebody in New York buys a kid a pair of pants or a shirt? If we don't take positive steps, that's one thing. If we've made no effort at all to inform our alumni—and we have—that's when we deserve to get spanked."

Though Kehoe insists it is important to have active, interested, informed, and knowledgeable alumni, he would prefer that most of them stay out of the recruiting wars and help him fight the battle to meet the budget.

Maryland's annual athletic budget in 1973, for example, ran approximately $2.2 million, with 40 per cent of the funds provided from the $35 activity fee paid by every student on campus. The difference had to be made up in gate receipts and contributions.

In August 1970 Kehoe hired former marine colonel Tom Fields to administer the Maryland Education Foundation, an organization used exclusively to secure scholarship money for the athletic department. When Fields took over, the school was raising a little over $30,000 a year thanks to donations by 290 loyal supporters.

"North Carolina and North Carolina State were raising

over $500,000 at that point. We weren't even close," says Fields, who calls himself "the coach of the money team around here."

That first year, Fields set up five different categories for contributions, ranging from the "Lifetime Diamondback," a one-time, $10,000 contribution, to the Silver Program, a $100 gift per year. All donations, of course, were tax-deductible.

The Diamondback plan called for an annual contribution of $1,000 or more. Each member received a small gold Terrapin—the school's turtle-like logo—with an inlaid diamond. More important, the donor also was given four season tickets to all home football and basketball games, with an option to purchase eight tickets for the annual Atlantic Coast Conference basketball tournament.

In 1973 Fields had one $10,000 donor he declined to identify. There were 61 Diamondback givers and he raised $250,000. In 1974 more than 1,100 contributed in excess of $360,000 to the fund. Four hundred people gave $500 or more and there were six $10,000 donors. Half the contributors were not Maryland graduates. Fields set his goal for 1975 at $500,000.

Most schools supporting major-college athletics have similar programs. Arizona's $1,000-a-year donors receive the option to buy 10 football and basketball season tickets, parking in choice locations, a Wildcat Club golf sweater, a personalized plaque and car decal, and all publicity newsletters and press guides.

The dues for membership in the Cardinal and Gold, Southern Cal's most prestigious alumni group, are a $500 minimum. At Clemson, money is raised by the IPTAY Club. IPTAY was organized in 1934, and now stands for "I Pay Twenty a Year." (Three years ago, inflation forced a name change from "I Pay Ten a Year.")

All the money raised by the Maryland Education Foundation is used for athletic scholarships. Contrary to popular belief, a school simply cannot afford to allow a gifted athlete to attend free. The money for his scholarship—approximately $3,000 a year at Maryland, $4,000 a year at Southern Cal, and $5,000 a year at Harvard—is paid by the athletic department.

Without question, the number and amount of contributions often hinge on the athletic fortunes of the institution. The week after Virginia Tech won the 1973 NIT basketball tournament in Madison Square Garden, its president reported a phenomenal number of cash contributions.

Two months after North Carolina State won the 1974 NCAA basketball championship, well over $1 million in contributions had poured into the coffers of the Wolfpack Club, State's athletic scholarship fund. That represented twice the amount received the previous year, when the club had collected the largest sum in the history of the school.

The chief wolf's name is Warren Carroll, and he says, quite frankly, "You sit me down with a man and give me 30 minutes. I'll tell you how much he's going to give. How will I do that? Well, before I've gone into that man's office, I'll have learned everything I possibly can know about him.

"In this business, you've got to know your people and work them to the best of your ability."

There are now over 8,000 members of the Wolfpack Club, though only 50 per cent are State alumni. As long as their money is green and their checks don't bounce, it hardly matters.

"We have 66 people who annually give in excess of $1,000," Carroll said in March 1974. "We have 190 who gave an even $1,000. They're not all old people. In fact, I say the young people are taking over. I have one fellow who is 26 years old and gave $10,000 last year and also started paying $1,000 a month for a $25,000 life membership.

"I've heard we have the most successful club in the country," Carroll continued. "But I think something like this would work anywhere. To me, it's the most amazing thing that you can read stories in the *Wall Street Journal* about schools that just can't maintain their athletic programs. I can't believe it."

Why are alumni and synthetic alumni so loose with their cash? "They want something to boast about at their cocktail parties," says Bob Cousy.

"I think the main reason is the pride in belonging to a successful organization," says Jack Heise, a Silver Spring, Maryland, attorney and past president of the Maryland Alumni Association. "Alumni do get turned on. They do get turned on by winners. Anything I'm associated with, I want to be first. I want Maryland to be No. 1 in football and No. 1 in basketball. So I do whatever they ask me to."

It also makes good business sense. College-town merchants usually are more than happy to contribute to a school's athletic program, either with legitimate donations or direct gifts to the athletes themselves. The better a team does on the field, the more people will attend the games. The more people who attend the games, the more money is spent in a town's hotels, restaurants, and liquor stores.

On football Saturdays the city of Ann Arbor, Michigan, almost doubles its size when 100,000-plus fans jam into the football stadium, most of them coming from around the state. Thousands of free-spending Texans and Oklahomans pour into Dallas each year for the annual Oklahoma-Texas football game. Usually they stay from Friday until Sunday afternoon. The amount of money spent on booze alone is staggering.

Chuck Dekeado graduated from Syracuse in the late 1950s, but when his company transferred him to California he switched allegiances and became a loyal fan—and occasional recruiter—for Southern Cal.

He says he became so emotionally involved before USC football games that "I'd throw up, just worrying about whether they were going to win or lose." He once swallowed his cigar as he jumped to his feet to cheer a particularly gratifying O. J. Simpson touchdown run, the one that went for 64 yards and helped beat UCLA in 1967.

"What I didn't like," says Dekeado, who now helps Southern Cal football coach John McKay run his lucrative summer camp, "was the hate you had to develop for other schools. If somebody mentioned UCLA, Stanford, or Cal, my back would curl up like a cat."

Maryland's Heise also occasionally helps his alma mater recruit a youngster. If a boy shows an interest in a law career, Heise usually will be asked to speak with him or his parents. He also can arrange a summer job for a prospective student-athlete. If a Maryland player wants to buy a car, Heise can send him to an alumnus or a friend of the university "to give the kid advice," and probably a good deal as well. The Maryland coaching staff, in fact, has 23 courtesy cars on loan at no cost to the school.

"But I think the role of alumni is overrated," Heise insists. "You hear so much about things going on, how much influence an alumnus may have had on a kid. At our place, a coach rarely asks alumni to come along when he's getting the order book out, so to speak."

Still, many help considerably in the preliminary stages of recruiting. How does a youngster say no to a proposed campus visit when a senator, a governor, a professional quarterback makes the initial offer?

An exception was Dantley. When asked to dinner by Governor Mandel, a Maryland alumnus, Dantley politely declined. "That stuff doesn't appeal to me," he says.

Maryland basketball players Len Elmore and Jap Trimble, both from New York City, were recruited by Lefty Driesell's Manhattan connection, Sam Lefrak, landlord to a quarter of a million people in Brooklyn and Queens. A 1940 Maryland graduate who, by his own description, "puttered around running cross-country and the two-mile," Lefrak says, "Every once in a while they'll call and ask me to help them with a New York boy. I'm a very busy man, but I do what I can." Lefrak has phoned prospects, written them letters, visited their homes, and, more than occasionally, offered them summer jobs as construction workers for his firm. "And I make 'em work. They don't show up, they don't get paid."

Why does he bother?

"I still have a strong feeling for College Park. I find I still love the smell of grass in the state of Maryland. I still love D.C. I think it's our most beautiful city. So why shouldn't I tell a young lad to go there?

"I just use myself as an example. Mine is a success story. I've done a great deal. I've changed the skyline of New York. Look what Maryland did for me. Now I'd like to do something for Maryland.

"It's a fun thing for me. I haven't been to a football game in years, but I saw the basketball team when they played in the Garden. I look for the scores in the *Times*. When they win, I'm jubilant. When they lose, I'm depressed. I do what I can, that's all."

Lefrak's counterpart on the West Coast is Sam Gilbert, known simply as "Papa Sam" to UCLA's basketball players for more than a decade. The similarities between the two Sams are astonishing.

Both were children of the depression, both made their fortunes in the construction business, both are Jewish, and both take inordinate pride in their respective alma maters. While Lefrak rarely sees Maryland in action, Gilbert is assigned a permanent seat on the UCLA bench during home games, and rarely misses a contest home or away.

Ever since he convinced Kareem Abdul-Jabbar (then Lew Alcindor) and Lucius Allen not to transfer after their sophomore years—Abdul-Jabbar to Michigan and Allen to Kansas—Gilbert has played a vital and somewhat mysterious role in UCLA basketball.

Prugh and Chapin in *The Wizard of Westwood* call Gilbert "the man in the shadows. He is the last and most oblique of the four strong forces and counterforces in the John Wooden dynasty." Gilbert helped Jabbar negotiate his $1.4 million contract with the Milwaukee Bucks. Similarly, he has helped Allen, Sidney Wicks, Curtis Rowe, Steve Patterson, and Henry Bibby, among others, in their deliberations with the professionals. All "without asking for a dime," he says proudly.

In 1973 he handled all negotiations between the latest UCLA giant, Bill Walton, and the ABA and NBA teams after his considerable talents. Gilbert, in fact, had convinced the ABA to move its Carolina franchise to Los Angeles just so Walton would be able to stay and play in his beloved southern California. Walton eventually decided to take $2.8 million instead from the Portland Trailblazers.

If reporters ever wanted to speak with Walton, they phoned Gilbert, not the UCLA publicity department. Most of the time he kept the scribes away from the publicity-shy redhead. "Bill prefers not to have his privacy intruded upon," he once told a Washington *Post* reporter. "What would he say now anyway? He's been asked all the questions. Just leave him alone."

Gilbert and Lefrak differ in one major area. Gilbert steadfastly refuses to become involved in the recruiting of high school athletes. "I'm opposed to it unequivocally," he says. "It's degenerated into insanity. It's more important for a kid, especially a black kid, to get an education. When these recruiters pursue these kids with money, when they alter grades on transcripts, when they doctor test results, it's disgusting. They asked me a long time ago to talk to a young man, and I refused. They haven't asked me since." Instead Gilbert advises the players once they arrive on campus, and occasionally he does more. Alcindor frequently studied in Gilbert's twelfth-floor office in a room with a view of the San Fernando Valley below.

"I don't do it so much because I'm a UCLA alumnus," Gilbert says. "I'm like a chastity belt. You know what the agents are like, their rip-offs are legion. It's a question of keeping a level of dignity. I'd like to bring some semblance of morality into the athletic community."

At still another Big Ten school athletes quickly learned that one local wealthy businessman (an alumnus) in particular was a fellow well worth knowing. An All-America player and topflight professional verified the following incidents at his school both to a reporter on a metropolitan midwestern newspaper and to the authors of this book, but insisted that his name not be used under any circumstances. "I've got nothing really against the university," he said, "but if I state the facts about what happened, they always make it seem like I'm trying to knock the school and the state. When you're in a position where you don't have the power, you're in trouble. This whole last year, you should have seen the articles they printed about me. It never came out the way it was supposed to be. I just don't want to get involved in a verbal situation. I've got more sense than that."

This athlete confirmed that he had received money for the rent of an apartment that went beyond what the NCAA legally allowed its member institutions to offer. He received furniture sent his way by the alumnus, who never asked payment.

During his senior year, he said, his mother and two sisters were flown from their home in New York City to the Midwest to see him play. His mother said the tickets just came in the mail one day. She had no idea who sent them.

He also said he received an allowance of $75 a month. During his senior year he lived in an apartment and paid rent of $155 a month. He also leased a 1974 car for $130 a month.

"The rent was the biggest thing they usually paid," he said. "The rent came through the basketball coach. I would go to him to get my rent money. . . . I was told if I needed anything, there were people I could go to to get it." He said the coach told him that, too.

When the player was being recruited, the alumnus apparently was actively involved. "He told me anytime my parents or anyone in my family needed anything, all I had to do was ask. He would send it to them.

"He must have thought this would influence me some," he said, "which it didn't. I'd already made up my mind to go to this school. And I never asked about my family until my senior year, just to find out if he was telling the truth. He wasn't telling the truth. It was just like a recruiting gimmick."

The player added, however, that the alumnus gave him $200 the first time he met him on his recruiting trip to the school's campus. The alumnus also offered to send him on a vacation to Hawaii before he started school in 1971, but he declined to take the trip.

He also said he saw nothing wrong with accepting extras from the alumnus or anyone else.

"In a sense, it's like a semipro thing," he said. "You're getting paid. They give you the tuition, room, and board to play ball for the school.

"You are putting money into the school's pocket. As a matter of fact, as I see it, you repay the school.

"We repaid the school a number of times the amount of tuition and room and board and even if the guys get a little extra because we did sell out the place a number of times."

The authors attempted several times to contact the alumnus for comment. On the first attempt, he asked what the subject of the conversation would be.

"Recruiting," he was told. "We'd like to know what you do to help the program."

"Be glad to talk to you, but I'm kind of tied up right now. Give your name and phone number to my secretary and I'll call you back first thing in the morning."

Five mornings passed without a return call. Another call was placed to his office. This time the secretary had a brief message.

"Mr. Smith [a pseudonym] asked me to tell you that he hasn't been involved in recruiting for quite some time now and doesn't feel it would be at all worthwhile to speak with you."

A loyal alumnus to the end.

11 / The Unhappy Ones

JAMES MONROE, a marvelously gifted forward from Washington, D.C.'s McKinley High School, had heard all those stories about the University of Detroit and its tempestuous basketball coach, Jim Harding. One wily recruiter from another school had even provided the 6-foot-5 senior with excerpts from *Foul.* "Harding," wrote David Wolf, "had left a trail of NCAA violations, ineligible athletes, altered transcripts, tortuous three-hour practices, player resignations, and endless turmoil" while head coach at LaSalle in Philadelphia.

James Monroe read all of that in the summer of 1972, and still was not convinced. Certainly his high school coach couldn't provide much help. McKinley Armstrong, in addition to his duties as head basketball coach, also served as an assistant principal at the school, Washington's largest high school in the inner city. He barely had time to make all the practices and the games.

Once, when Monroe missed a crucial game in the 1972 season, Armstrong was asked why his star player had been absent. "It's his business, not mine," the coach replied. "I don't know where he is, and I haven't had time to find out."

He also had little time to help Monroe select a college, so the youngster headed out for Detroit in the fall of 1972. Three months later he was back home, another recruiting victim.

Monroe's problems began a few weeks after he arrived on the university's urban campus. He injured his knee in a preseason workout, and argued with Harding over the advisability of practicing while injured. Finally he quit the team. The coach, whom a Philadelphia writer once described as "Baron Von Harding," had struck again.

Harding insists that Monroe saw two university physicians who told him rest would be of no value in rehabilitating his knee. "He would have had to play above it," says the coach, who has since resigned his post and retired from active coaching. "He chose not to play. We made no effort to talk him back into playing. If a boy doesn't want to play, that's his decision."

"Yeah, a lot of people told me about him," Monroe admitted after returning home. I sure found out. I should have listened, I made a bad mistake."

And so, too, do countless thousands of other high school athletes. For every David Thompson or Bill Walton who lead their respective schools to the promised land of huge gate receipts and national championships, there are untold numbers of recruiting victims.

Most can usually be seen sitting on the team bench, a few seats down from the men who once promised them the world to entice them to their schools, then simply recruited someone better.

But more than occasionally, these disgruntled, disillusioned athletes never make it to the stadiums or arenas of America's major-college programs. Like Monroe, who never played in a University of Detroit basketball game, they transfer to another school or drop out completely, never to be heard from again.

"We're dealing with kids, and a lot of them, especially the inner-city ones, don't have a realistic idea what college is all about," says Georgetown coach John Thompson. "Not enough kids in the city have exposure. They think college is going to be one great adventure. They don't realize they're going to have a difficult time adjusting. Somebody's got to tell these kids, 'Hey, it's going to be rough.' Everybody gives them advice when they're making the choice, but they take the trip back home all by themselves."

Monroe was one of the fortunate ones. He went back to Washington after dropping out of school, and worked for a while in the post office. In the summer of 1973 he got in touch with Terry Truax, a Florida assistant who had once coached him in high school.

Unable to get him into Florida, Truax called his friend Bobby Hussey, the head coach at tiny Belmont Abbey in North Carolina. Hussey had recruited Monroe out of high school, and was only too thrilled at getting a second chance to get him back in school.

Monroe sat out the 1973–74 season as required by the NCAA of all transfer students. "But he practiced with us every day, worked real hard at it," says Hussey. "He'll be our starting forward next season. He's got no problems here, I guarantee that."

Many of Monroe's contemporaries never had his good fortune, however. In a 1973 survey of its All-Metropolitan teams of the previous four years, the Washington *Post* reported that 35 per cent of its selections no longer were playing college basketball, though every player had been enrolled on a full basketball scholarship as a freshman.

All of them were highly recruited by the nation's junior colleges and universities. Some of the dropouts, like Monroe, didn't get along with their college coaches; others suffered injuries. Two homesick players lasted less than a week of their first semesters.

One of those players was Charles Campbell, who took Ballou High School to the Washington public school playoffs in 1971, and led the city in scoring with a 28-point average. He was a 6-3 guard, and thought nothing of putting the ball up from 25 feet. Usually, he connected.

The same could not be said of his prowess in the classroom. Several major schools were interested until they received copies of his high school transcript and College Board scores. Virginia Union, a small black school in Richmond, offered him a basketball scholarship.

When Campbell arrived on campus in the fall of 1971, he went to register for classes and was told he still owed the school $550. The sum was to have been paid by a federal grant because he came from a family with a yearly income of less than $6,000.

"All he had to do was go downstairs and sign for the money," says Virginia Union basketball coach Thomas Harris. "He just didn't take the time to do it. He left. He never even talked to me."

"When they told me I owed the money," says Campbell, "I called my mother. I knew she didn't have the money. She's on social security. We got eight kids in the family. It would take three monthly checks to pay that. What are the others supposed to do, starve?

"I went and talked to an assistant coach, and he said

there was some kind of mixup. I was just worried they wouldn't give me my scholarship. So I came home. I was kind of mad."

Campbell then enrolled at Prince George's Community College in suburban Maryland. He withdrew 21 days later, he says, because the Virginia Union people had called back and told him he could return for the second semester.

But Charles Campbell never went back. He didn't want to leave his common-law wife and his 17-month-old daughter, and he was not all that crazy about continuing his academic career.

In January 1972 Campbell was offered a full scholarship to attend Langston University in Oklahoma, another small black school, 35 miles from Oklahoma City. He visited one weekend, arriving on a Saturday and leaving the following Monday. He told the coach, Glenn Gibson, he wanted to come to school and would be back after returning to Washington to straighten out a car accident. His car apparently had been stolen, he told Gibson, and then was cracked up. The police had issued a warrant for his arrest when the driver fled the accident scene.

Campbell never went back to Langston. He never even called to say he wasn't coming. "I was going to take care of him, get him in school, get him playing for us as soon as he registered," Gibson recalls. "Then he went home. I left half a dozen messages for him to call me. Then I gave up. It was obvious that if the boy wanted to come out here, he would have called."

Campbell says he didn't call because he didn't particularly care for Oklahoma. He also was working on a plan to get a package scholarship deal for himself and his little brother Randolph, who would be graduating in the spring of 1972.

Randolph Campbell, though five inches shorter than his brother, was just as deadly on the basketball court. He, too, was named to the All-Metropolitan team, after a senior year in which he averaged 25 points and seven assists a game for Ballou.

"It just looks to me now like Charles is trying to muscle in on Randy," said his high school coach, Herman Daves. "But people aren't going to buy any package deal." And he was absolutely correct. Randolph, in fact, did not attend any school at all in the fall of 1972. He worked, instead, in the post office.

Daves did finally convince Randolph to at least try college, and managed to get him a scholarship to Ranger Junior College in Ranger, Texas, that would start in January 1973.

"He lasted three days," says Ranger coach Ron Butler. "He couldn't play because we already were in the middle of the season and he was ineligible. He just said he couldn't stand to be there and not be playing. Of course, we're a long way from home for him, too. I'm sure that also had something to do with it."

Interviewed shortly after returning from Texas, Randolph said he didn't particularly care to talk about his experiences at Ranger because he had recently enrolled at Johnson C. Smith College in Charlotte, North Carolina.

But the coach at the school, Joe Alston, said he had never even heard of Randolph Campbell. "I know everybody in my program," he said. "Maybe he played intramurals or something." The Johnson C. Smith Registrar's office did not list a Randolph Campbell on its records. Three Campbells were registered at the school, two from South Carolina and another from North Carolina. Randolph Campbell, it seemed, had never gone to school there. He was still working in the post office. In 1973 he enrolled at Washington's Federal City College, but he never played on the basketball team.

Charles, meanwhile, worked a variety of odd jobs and did some construction work. Contacted in the summer of 1974, he said he was planning to enroll at "some school in North Carolina." His brother, he said, was going to transfer from Federal City to a school in Wisconsin.

"We've been playin' on the playground all the time," Charles Campbell said. "I want to go back to school, but you know how it is, man. Maybe I'll go in the fall. You never know what's gonna happen. Biggest mistake I ever made was leaving Virginia Union. But that's life."

He stood there, that brutally oppressive summer day in August 1972, manacled to an attendant in a Montgomery County, Maryland, courthouse. Dressed in blue jeans, a blue work shirt, tan lace-up shoes, and no socks, he faced Judge Joseph M. Mathias.

His name was Cyril Baptiste, and only a year earlier he had signed a contract to play professional basketball for the San Francisco Warriors. Under its terms, he was to receive $450,000 over four years. "Cyril," said Warrior publicist Harry Jupiter, "can no longer be considered a financial hardship case."

But now, 11 months later, he was about to be sentenced for arson, a charge that carried a maximum penalty of 30 years.

Cyril Baptiste's problems had started long before he was escorted into that courthouse, long before he had set fire to an apartment he was sharing with a friend.

One of four children raised by his widowed mother in a Miami ghetto, he had been a high school All-America at

Archbishop Curley High School in 1967, and was considered the most talented basketball player the city had ever produced. Over 100 schools were eager to obtain his services, but Baptiste, with more than a little help from his mother and his high school coach, wound up at Creighton, a small, 2,500-student Jesuit school in Omaha, Nebraska.

Baptiste's high school coach, Phil Petta, had once played for Red McManus, the Creighton coach at the time, and strongly influenced his star player to attend his alma mater. Mrs. Baptiste, a strict Catholic who guided her flock to church each Sunday and many days in between, also liked the idea of her son keeping close to the faith and playing basketball, too.

If Cyril had had his own way, he would have preferred to attend Texas–El Paso. He fell in love with the school and its program on his campus visit, and he liked the climate. Still, he also wanted to make his mother happy and proud, so he signed a letter-of-intent to attend Creighton.

Baptiste was academically ineligible his freshman year because of poor high school grades. Then, in the spring of 1969, McManus and the school "parted ways by mutual agreement," according to the former coach, now the prosperous owner of a tuxedo rental business in Omaha.

"Cyril had everthing," McManus says. "He had more potential than any other player we ever had at Creighton. I only wish I could have been around to coach him."

Baptiste was miserable at Creighton, according to several sources at the school. "We know Cyril had a lot of problems and that he wasn't happy here," says Dan Offenburger, chairman of the school's physical education department and Baptiste's academic adviser. "He wasn't cut out for this kind of school. He was a long way from home, and he hated the weather. A kid who comes here has to have a deep-seated academic interest. And Cyril never did."

Baptiste nevertheless returned for his sophomore season, and played well, averaging 19 points and 12 rebounds a game. Still, there were rumors that Baptiste "was fooling around with drugs," according to Eddie Sutton, the man who replaced McManus as Creighton's head coach.

Were the rumors true? Those close to Baptiste offered their respective appraisals.

"You never would have known it the way Cyril played for us," Sutton insists. "But then I really began to suspect something his junior year. He wasn't playing very well, and toward the end of the season he was losing a lot of weight. We gave him physicals, but they never turned up anything."

"It seemed rather difficult to believe they didn't notice anything," said Lew Schaffel, his lawyer-agent.

"When I was shooting heroin," Baptiste told Neil Amdur of *The New York Times*, "that's all I thought about—when my next shot was coming, how I could get it. The school carried me through on some grades, especially when I got strung out."

Certainly Baptiste's performance on the court gave Creighton enough reason to keep him eligible. He averaged 20 points and 11 rebounds a game his junior season, and was named to several All-America teams.

"It just shows you what a super athlete the kid was," says Jim Morse, his attorney in the Maryland arson case. "He actually played a year of college basketball on drugs. Two years really."

"I probably will never get another ballplayer with that much ability," says Sutton. "All Cyril lived for, though, was to play professional basketball. He was a very confused young man, but I always thought he had a lot of good in him. He had bad habits. He was an amazing sleeper, impossible to wake up. So he was always late for practice.

"He was a moody player, too. He always played well against teams like Marquette, our bigger games. He always played up to the competition. Don't get me wrong. He's a great player. I don't think he would have been a superstar, but I know he would have been an outstanding pro basketball player."

Two weeks after his junior basketball season had ended, Baptiste left Creighton "for academic reasons," according to Offenburger. Other sources indicated that the school had finally become aware of his drug problem, and since he was doing poorly in class and the basketball season had ended, he was advised to withdraw.

The Warriors knew about Baptiste's problems when they signed him in the hardship draft. In September 1971 he went to training camp with the team, and was "clean," according to his attorney, Jerry Davis. "He had cut out the drugs. The first two days at camp were fine," Davis says, "and then somehow he got hooked up with some guy out there and started with drugs again. I don't know what was in his psyche to do it again. It was a good situation for him. But something snapped.

"At that point we started getting calls, some of them at midnight, from the Warriors. Cyril left camp, then came back—all sorts of weird things. The first week of camp they put him under medication and he missed a week or 10 days. Then he came back and worked out. He stayed with the club all during the exhibition season, but he wasn't in good condition. I think the longest he played was six minutes.

"We made several contract adjustments with the Warriors, and they kept him until the day the season started, when it became obvious he couldn't do anything for them until he resolved his problem."

"It was a sad case," says Bob Feerick, the Warriors'

general manager. "He was a sick kid, that's all you could say. . . . We did everything we could for him."

Baptiste left the Warriors, and, ashamed to go home to Miami, went to Washington, D.C., where his sister Bernadette worked for the FBI. Schaffel and Davis, his representatives, persuaded a friend, Jack Schore, to let Baptiste stay at his apartment and take treatment at the Narcotics Treatment Administration.

In November, less than a month after being released by San Francisco, Baptiste was arrested and charged with arson for setting a fire in Schore's apartment, and with grand larceny for taking a television set and stereo equipment, all belonging to Schore. He was released on personal recognizance, and resumed attending sessions at the Narcotics Treatment Administration while awaiting trial.

Baptiste stayed in the program until the NTA thought he was cured, and in January he left for Miami. A few weeks later he returned to Washington. Apparently, he still was hooked.

On May 10, 1972, Baptiste was arrested by District of Columbia police as he walked down a corridor in the posh Statler Hilton hotel, testing doors to see if they were unlocked. Baptiste was given a 180-day suspended sentence, with 18 months of strict narcotics surveillance, on that offense.

On June 21 he was found guilty of the arson charge in Montgomery County, and unable to post $500 bail, he went to jail to await sentencing. Six weeks later Judge Mathias gave him a three-year sentence and placed him on probation, "to give you a chance to make good." The judge also imposed four conditions on Baptiste's probation: that he live with his mother in Miami; that he "diligently condition" himself to play basketball, and also seek employment in order to support himself; that he eventually seek to gain employment as a professional basketball player, and if that became impossible, obtain employment in some other field; and that he refrain from contact with narcotics or other dangerous drugs and not associate with anyone who did.

"With all your potential you should be able to make good," the judge said. "Any defendant who appears to have some possibility of straightening out—to be salvageable—I'm willing to give a chance."

Baptiste flew home three days later. His attorneys tried in vain to get him another shot with a professional team, but no one in either league was interested. Baptiste apparently began getting involved with narcotics again, until he was befriended by Alan Goldfarb, a former all-city player from Miami Beach and an attorney.

In 1973, with Goldfarb's help, Baptiste enrolled in a drug rehabilitation center in Fort Lauderdale. He spent three and a half months there, attending therapy sessions from 10 A.M. to 10 P.M. every day. Again, he seemed cured. "I don't have to worry about shooting drugs anymore," Baptiste said, when it was over. "I don't think about it anymore."

Goldfarb helped Baptiste join the Scranton Apollos in the Eastern Basketball League for the 1973–74 season. He played the entire year, averaged 12 points, and earned $150 a game.

"Cyril can play in the NBA," said George Wyatt, a part-owner of the East Orange Colonials, another Eastern League team. "Right now [the spring of 1974] he's good enough to make any pro team. When he tries out this summer, if they let him, somebody's gonna have to sit down."

But that is the problem. Schaffel and Davis, who still represent Baptiste, so far have been unable to convince any teams to take a chance on their troubled client. "You can't really blame them," says Schaffel. "He's been cured in the past and gone back. But I really believe Cyril has come out of this thing all right.

"The thing that bothers me is that all of this could have been avoided. He made one bad decision in his life, to go to Creighton, and look what happened because of it. If only he'd gone to UTEP. . . ."

"It's so sad," says Morse, his Maryland attorney. "Here's a kid who's been used all his life because he was a great basketball player. He's a gentle guy, not violent at all, and definitely a warm, friendly person.

"He was captured by drugs. The devil owned his soul."

In 1971 Rudy Jackson was shooting basketballs with as much proficiency as Cyril Baptiste was shooting junk into his veins. Jackson was 6-foot-10, weighed 220 pounds, and could hit with deadly accuracy from the far perimeters of a basketball court.

"Yeah, I learned to shoot out on the playgrounds when I was a little kid," he says. "I was always taller than most of my friends, and I felt bad about taking them to the hoop and muscling it up. So I just started shooting outside so they'd let me keep playing with them."

In his senior year at Bowne High School in Queens, Jackson was the scourge of the New York public school leagues and was named to the all-city team. But, like so many inner-city black athletes, he had atrocious grades, and his college options were extremely limited.

In high school, Jackson had been befriended by Steve Shalin, a former Bowne graduate and a young man who had organized a basketball team called the Salukis and stocked it with promising ghetto players. Jackson was one of them. So were Len Elmore, John Shumate and Billy Schaeffer, all now in the pros.

"He used to help guys out, call up schools and see if they were interested, that kind of thing," Jackson recalls. "Steve was my friend. I trusted him completely. Maybe I trusted him too much."

Shalin called up the people at Wichita State in 1971 and helped them arrange for Jackson to attend Hutchinson Junior College in Kansas. Jackson would stay there a year, improve his high school grades, then transfer to Wichita State the following year. In return for his help, Wichita State coach Harry Miller gave Shalin, then 23, a scholarship and made him a student-assistant in the basketball program.

Shalin supplied both schools, Hutchinson and Wichita State, with copies of Jackson's high school transcript, which showed that he had graduated from Bowne High, though both the coach and the player knew better.

Officials at Hutchinson had no reason to suspect that Jackson was considerably short of credits to graduate from high school, and they admitted him the following fall. That season Jackson averaged 25 points and 21 rebounds a game, led Hutchinson to the finals of the national junior college basketball tournament, and was named to the juco All-America team. The Indiana Pacers of the American Basketball Association even drafted him on the second round of their undergraduate draft.

Jackson took 24 credits at Hutchinson and maintained a C average there, so there was no difficulty at all in transferring to Wichita State the following fall. He still would be playing collegiate basketball if Mickey Holmes, the commissioner of the Missouri Valley Conference, in a routine check of records, hadn't discovered that Jackson had not graduated from Bowne High School.

"He's a beautiful person," Shalin told Steve Jacobson of *Newsday.* "That's why I did what I did. To see him destroyed by the system would be wrong. I told him, 'Don't let anyone know what a stinkin' student you are.'

"I had 150 blank checks from colleges for him. No one cared about his grades, including Wichita State. Including me. He had coaches with white shoes telling him all he had to do was show up. All he had to do was graduate from high school.

". . . So I walked into the office [at Bowne] when it was empty, changed grades to indicate graduation, and had the transcript sent."

"The first I learned about the Jackson situation was when I was contacted by the admissions people at Wichita," Harvey Katz, Bowne's acting principal, said last year. "I saw the transcript and it took me about two minutes to determine it was a phony.

"The first thing that struck me was that his grades were typed in. We write ours in because we send out about 800 a year and it's quicker to write the grades. Also, his grade in economics was 75. I was his teacher for that course, and I recall giving him 65.

"I wish these recruiters would leave the kids alone until they graduate. Rudy was a nice boy. Not the best of students, but a fine citizen in our school. He was short a good deal of credits for graduation. It was not something he could make up over the summer. We expected him to return in the fall of 1972, but when he never did, we just discharged him. He was over 17, and he can leave school at that age."

"At no time did we have doubts that Rudy had graduated from high school," said Sam Butterfield, the athletic director at Hutchinson. "All his papers and everything the Wichita people told us indicated he had. We take people from 18 to 80 here, and our only requirement is a high school diploma."

As soon as Wichita State was informed that Jackson had not yet graduated from high school, it declared him ineligible for the 1973–74 basketball season. It also dismissed Shalin, who was receiving $100 a month and free tuition. He was nine credits short of graduation. All of this occurred in October 1973, and Shalin disappeared soon after. He is now living in Houston, Texas, and working for a personnel concern.

"I've never taken a penny for a player," Shalin said. I told Rudy, if you don't make it in education, I'm finished with basketball. He didn't and I quit . . . I'm rich for what I did. I can sleep at night."

The Missouri Valley Conference placed Wichita State on two-year probation. The school will be able to continue playing basketball, but has been barred from any postseason tournament appearances. The NCAA also investigated, and added its own two-year probation.

Jackson was stripped of his athletic scholarship, though Wichita State athletic director Ted Bredahoft said he tried to convince the player to stay in school in "the hope we could have gotten him eligible for next season. I really thought we could.

"The thing that really bothers me about this whole business is that there was no need to falsify his transcript. Even if Rudy hadn't graduated from high school, he could have taken that G.E.D. [General Education Development] test. If he passed, it wouldn't have mattered about the diploma."

What of Jackson's role in the whole affair? Certainly he knew that he was not eligible to graduate from high school, that in order to play college basketball he needed a diploma.

"Steve told me he would take care of everything," Jackson said in a recent interview. "He told me not to worry, 'cause he knew how to get around those kind of things. Like I said, I trusted the dude. We were tight, real good friends. Why shouldn't I have believed what he said? I didn't know any better."

Jackson told Wichita State's Bredahoft basically the same story, and though the athletic director sympathized with his predicament, he noted, "Rudy had some involvement in this thing, too. He did sign our admissions application that asks, very specifically, 'Did you graduate from high school?' He knew he didn't, but he signed anyway.

"But I'm not angry at Rudy. He had bad guidance. We're not entirely blameless either, and we're paying for it. I am just very sorry that Steve Shalin ever got involved in our program. We thought he could help us. He had good contacts back in New York City, and we thought he could get us good players. But we didn't want him to cheat to do it.

"We regret the incident very much."

Jackson went to Baton Rouge, Louisiana, after leaving Wichita State and played in the national AAU championships before he broke his foot in a semifinal game. He returned to his parents' home in South Jamaica, New York, in the spring of 1974, was drafted by the New York Knicks in the third round, and signed for $80,000.

Jackson had other memorable experiences on the recruiting trails, and one day in the spring of 1974 he talked about them in the living room of his parents' home on 110th Street. It was a quiet, tree-lined street of detached houses. The lawns were neatly trimmed, and spring flowers were just starting to make an appearance.

Jackson's smile lit up the living room as he recalled the $10,000 in cash offered by an owner of a Las Vegas casino if he would sign that afternoon to attend Nevada-Las Vegas; another school sending a prostitute to his room, promising to pay off his parents' mortgage, and offering to give him a car; South Carolina asking, "Who's your favorite player on the Knicks?", then offering to have Walt Frazier, Jackson's favorite, show up the next day; a Big Eight coach offering a $10,000 trust fund if Jackson would sign. "When I said no," Jackson recalled, "the guy was practically down on his knees begging. He kept asking, 'What do we have to do? What do we have to do?' I couldn't believe it."

Jackson also once told LSU basketball coach Dale Brown and the school's assistant publicist, Jerry Walker, that a southern assistant coach had offered his parents $20,000 if he would come to the man's school. His parents politely asked the recruiter to leave the house.

When contacted a month later, Jackson declined further comment on his recruiting experiences. "My lawyers don't want me to talk about it," he said. "Just say this. Just say it's a dirty, rotten business. There's a lot of people out there taking advantage of people like me. I'm lucky. I got another chance and I think I can play pro ball. But there's a lot of dudes running around on the streets been screwed bad, real bad. What's gonna happen to them?"

What indeed. There now follows the story of what happened to an entire class of football players at the University of Maryland, a school that won the national championship in 1953, then faded far from national prominence in the late 1960s. The class we studied was recruited with the hope of rebuilding another power in the 1970s.

12 / The Survivors

NOVEMBER 24, 1973, had been the most glorious day for Maryland football in 18 years, and it ended, appropriately enough, with the seniors standing above their teammates and leading a robust rendition of the school fight song.

In the corridor outside the plush, ecstatic dressing room were jammed dozens of burly and swift high school prospects, some of whom undoubtedly were influenced by the enthusiasm during and after the 42-9 rout of Tulane to sign grants-in-aid and dream of even greater glory for Maryland and Coach Jerry Claiborne—and for themselves.

Had they noticed, during the euphoria of Maryland's first bowl team since the glory years of Jim Tatum, the seniors immediately would have grasped the irony of the scene. Later, all in fact did recall their four-year experience, how tiring and painful it had been, how bleak the future often seemed, and how many of the players who came with them were not on hand for the singing.

Four years before, Maryland had signed 29 prospects to scholarships. Two, Chris Carter and Dave Begacki, never arrived. Of the remaining 27, only 11 were still playing football at Maryland four years later. Of those 11, there were 4—offensive linemen Cy Jernigan and Bart Purvis, quarterback Al Neville, and defensive lineman Paul Vellano—who graduated on time.

The coach who recruited them, Roy Lester, had been fired two years earlier.

Seven of those 11 players—Neville, Jernigan, receiver Dan Bungori, guard Purvis, and fullback Monte Hinkle on offense and linemen Vellano and Ken Scott on defense—all cornerstones of a team that compiled Maryland's best record since 1955, were seniors.

The other four—blockers Frank Romano and Stan Rogers and defenders Ed Serembus and Steve Zannoni—still had a year of football eligibility remaining.

But there were so many more who came in the fall of 1970, fresh and confident, only to quit under the pressures, pain, and politics of major-college football or to transfer to other schools. The cost included bitterness and frustration as well as thousands of wasted scholarship dollars.

College football demands up to five hours most days, and, as Bungori explains so well, "Everybody loves the game on Saturday but it's hard to love it Monday through Friday." Very few players are able to excel athletically, academically, and socially, and even fewer have never considered quitting during that dreadful combination of post-practice pain and an important exam the next morning.

"One night I headed for the Beltway, and I must have driven an hour mulling it all over—not getting a chance to play and all," says Romano, who did not quit.

"It seemed like all the fun had left," says Bob Abbott,

who did. "It got to be too much business. I was too tired to study or go to class. My grades were hurting." Four years after receiving a scholarship—and giving it up—Abbott was a second-semester sophomore.

For the Romanos and Vellanos who stayed, and for athletic director Jim Kehoe, there had been individual distinction in addition to helping the Terrapins to their first winning season since 1964.

"I've been waiting five years for this, five miserable damn years," said Kehoe after the Tulane rout. His fist was punching air and his mind was racing backward to another time when Maryland was ranked nationally—among the 20 worst teams in the country.

One is uncertain just when Maryland football struck bottom, because it seemed to reach unimagined depths with each season. Clearly, there was no lower time than the first week in March 1969, when Kehoe, who was then acting athletic director, presided over a mutiny.

Maryland had been 4-6 under Lou Saban in 1966, and hopes were kindled until he abruptly left to build the Denver Broncos. The grittiest—and perhaps best—player Maryland ever produced, Bob Ward, succeeded Saban.

It is difficult to imagine anyone working harder—or being more loyal—than Ward. But very little went right. Maryland experienced the worst record in its history, 0-9, his first year and was 2-8 his second. Then the players presented a list of grievances to Kehoe and Ward was out less than a week later.

At the time Kehoe said he wanted a coach "who can get along with young men," and he immediately turned to Roy Lester, whose teams at nearby Richard Montgomery High had compiled an 86-10-1 record.

Lester was Maryland's fourth coach in five years, prompting opposition recruiters to suggest to prospects that the Terrapins actually had three coaches: one coming, one going, and one on the field.

Maryland had cramped facilities, little stability, and a football tradition reduced to a memory. But Lester and his chief recruiter, Dim Montero, were persuasive fellows and, in their first full year, signed a class of 29 rich in size and talent.

Although Carter, a runner from Annapolis, failed to qualify academically and Begacki, a quarterback from Woodbury, New Jersey, accepted a baseball contract from the Atlanta Braves, the class included nine high school All-Americas. They were:

Quarterback Al Neville, from Bel Air, Maryland, who broke a national passing record with 59 touchdowns and 4,935 yards in 1968–69.

Running back Lem James, from New Canaan, Connecticut, who averaged eight yards a carry and broke many of Floyd Little's records despite playing just half of several games.

Linebacker-running back Bob Gawler, from Lester's Richard Montgomery, the outstanding player in the Washington area.

Flanker Bob Lane, from Glen Ridge, New Jersey, who scored 108 points on an undefeated team.

Tight end Brent Sanford, from Derby, Connecticut, 6-foot-4 and 250 pounds, whose coach said he was the best college prospect he had seen in 25 years.

Linebacker Wayne Thornhill, from Ellwood City, Pennsylvania, so outstanding in a talent-rich area of western Pennsylvania that his jersey was retired.

Defensive lineman Paul Vellano, from Schenectady, New York, Scholastic and Parade All-America team.

Lineman Ken Scott, from Bricktown, New Jersey, so good even Texas recruited him.

Tackle Stan Rogers, from Pottstown, Pennsylvania, who was recruited by Penn State, Notre Dame, and 40 other schools.

Or at least that was how the Maryland coaches and recruiters described their catches at the time. Vellano recalls being somewhat surprised at learning he'd grown nearly 2 inches taller and about 20 pounds heavier the day he arrived at Maryland. And been recruited by about 30 more schools than he'd thought.

"Maryland was the only school that was seriously interested in me," he insists.

Still, Vellano is the one member of that class for whom all the dreams came true. His list of honors filled a third of a page in the Maryland football brochure and he became the school's first first-team All-America since Gary Collins 12 years earlier.

Neville, Scott, and Rogers achieved more modest success. Neville played splendidly at times, but also spent a frustrating amount of time on the sidelines with his arm in a sling.

Scott fell victim to a typical problem, position switching. He was moved from linebacker to defensive end to offensive tackle to defense, and then nearly back to offense again until a defensive right tackle quit in 1972. He was a regular there after that.

Rogers had a knee operation before he arrived at Maryland and missed his freshman season. No one told him he would be a blocker in college, but he became a superior offensive tackle.

"This [his experience at Maryland] taught me to be a disciplined person," says Neville. "I don't think I'll ever quit something."

These are the four high-school All-Americas who made the transition to major-college football, who arrived when Maryland was the Atlantic Coast Conference doormat, and who left when it had become one of the most respected teams in the nation.

The other five dropped out: Gawler before playing a game for Maryland, James and Lane after their freshman seasons, and Sanford and Thornhill after two years.

In three years at Derby High, Sanford had never played in a losing game. The Maryland freshman team lost its opener.

Bob Gawler played part of his senior year of high school with two broken wrists. A running back-linebacker, he was chosen the most outstanding player in the Washington area in 1969, then quit the Maryland team after a few weeks.

"At that point, the fun I got out of football just wasn't there," he says. "I was just tired of it. I wanted to study." Although others in his family feel differently, Gawler insists "I like Lester. He treated me fairly, although because I was so small [5-foot-9] he made it seem like I couldn't take the punishment after I left."

Six months after he dropped football, Gawler endured three operations to correct his high school injuries. He completed two years at Maryland, majoring in pre-dentistry, and accumulated a 3.4 average out of a possible 4.0. But finances were a problem and he dropped out of school, driving a cab and wondering if he could muster the money—and the inclination—to try college again.

There is general agreement among players who stayed and players who left that there was little discipline or organization on the freshman team, coached by Joe Gardi.

"We'd be running sprints and a lot of us would balk," says one player who stayed. "We were a pretty cocky bunch, and instead of saying 'Hey, recruiting's over, get to work' he'd just say 'All right, do it your way.' "

In addition, there were titters about some of the sideline

signals. When Gardi pointed inside his mouth, the offense was to run a trap. When he grabbed an imaginary broom and began dusting the sideline, the offense was to run a sweep. A shoveling motion meant a "dig," or straight-ahead plunge.

"I think the world of Joe Gardi," says Gary Shenton, who left Maryland after his freshman season and was working in his father's maintenance company in New Jersey three years later. "He was the one who took the time to come up and discuss the problems I had. He was really concerned."

A team never has enough linemen, and two of the biggest who entered Maryland in 1970 were 6-foot-8 Dave Clough and 260-pound Jim Boyle. Injuries caused an early end to both their careers.

"I played my freshman and sophomore years," says Clough, who is from Upland, Pennsylvania. "Then the first spring under coach Claiborne the [back] problems acted up. They began in high school. The operation to correct everything would have taken a whole day, and I'd have been immobile for six months. By that time, I figured, I'd either weigh 300 pounds or 165. I decided not to undergo surgery and finish out my education."

Clough retained his scholarship, assisting with the junior varsity. He graduated.

Boyle, from Levittown, Pennsylvania, started Maryland's 1971 season opener as a sophomore. Then the pain in his leg became unbearable.

"He was in the hospital five weeks, hopeful that an operation could cure things," says his father. "There was clotting. But the doctors said no surgical cure was possible and that any further participation in sports would be fatal."

Boyle eventually dropped out of Maryland, although his father said the school "bent over backward to honor his scholarship." He was working and attending Bucks County Community College two years later.

It was about midway through their freshman season that several of the new recruits began looking around and realizing that there were others at Maryland who could play football—that being the best in one high school, or one area, or even one state did not mean prominence at Maryland.

"The biggest thing I came to appreciate here was the second and third teamers," says Neville. "The starter knows he's going to get his four tickets and probably his name in the papers. Most important, he knows he's going to play Saturday and probably be recognized on campus. The second and third teamers hardly get any of it, just the knocks. Yet they keep coming out."

The biggest blow to a player is that there is someone better at his position—or someone the coaches *believe* is better. His ego is partially salved, though, if the team is successful, because he views himself as at least part of a winner. Maryland was 7-25 under Lester.

"For a while I was about the biggest thing in town," says Wayne Thornhill. "When I go back home now, some of the people really flip. 'You had the world by the tail, why didn't you stick it out?' they say. They don't realize that there's more important things than what I had to do as a football player."

Thornhill was raised in an area of western Pennsylvania that takes pride in the football players it produces, among them Joe Namath and Cookie Gilchrist.

But Thornhill began being pulled from football even before he reported to Maryland as a freshman. He lost 20 pounds during an illness, then became an 18-year-old father. After several injuries, Thornhill found himself on the scrubs in 1971, "holding dummies and taking everybody else's bruises." That continued and he quit a year later.

"It was a buildup of things," he says. "Day after day busting your butt and nothing happening, not getting the chance you deserved. You hurt so much, although you overlook that when you're playing. You know, you really can get hurt. And I wouldn't tell anyone to get married and play football."

During the Terrapins' return to prominence, Thornhill, who gave up his scholarship, was working as a mail carrier in nearby Greenbelt, trying to save enough money to resume his zoology studies at Maryland.

The most disillusioning aspect for the new recruits is what is known as "politics," players being switched from position to position by aides anxious to stock their special area. Lester maintains that the switching under his regime was to try to place a reasonably skilled player at each position, because he inherited very little talent.

The assistant coach who recruited Sam Martin left Maryland the summer of 1971, and, according to Martin, "I kinda got lost in the shuffle. I started at linebacker in spring practice, but when I came back in the fall I was about fifth team."

Four of the players quit primarily because of injuries: Lane (ankle), Dave Clough (back), Jim Boyle (leg), and Steve Kimball (ankle). Of those who quit for other reasons, most complained of too many restrictions, such as hair length and curfew, although Martin echoed the most serious charge.

"They promised such a good education when I was being recruited," he said. "They said the emphasis was on studies first and then football. But the first day we arrived at school we had a meeting and it was all turned around. He [Lester] said family was first, football was second, and studies were least important. I remember that."

"Football is a tough game, and a kid going to college has got to be a dedicated player and student," said Lester, who became football coach at a Maryland high school after being dismissed as Terrapin coach. "That's no bull. It's got to be that way. I don't know of a school in the country that treats its players better than at Maryland. Tutoring help is there, all a kid has to do is grab it."

The players said there has been an increased emphasis on academics under Claiborne.

Usually, Lester said, a player who transfers rarely plays anywhere else. Of the six players who transferred from Maryland—Sanford and James to Southern Connecticut, Martin and Shenton to Montclair (New Jersey) State, Tim Kostelnik to Slippery Rock, and Mark Daniels to Cincinnati—none are still playing. All switched to smaller schools near their hometowns.

Of the original class of 27 at Maryland, 22 still were in college four years later, with 17 of them at Maryland. Of the six nonplayers still at Maryland, Lane, Kimball, and Scott Loomis graduated on time.

Nationally, Penn State gave football scholarships to 24 prospects in 1970, and 18 were active four years later. Pitt's ratio was 17 of 31, North Carolina State's 13 of 26, Ohio State's 24 of 32, Texas's 30 of 45, Alabama's 27 of 38, and Indiana's 14 of 24. The figures do not include players injured but still on scholarship.

Of the nonstudents who quit Maryland, James was the assistant manager of a clothing store in Stamford, Connecticut; Jerry Stoll was a driver-salesman for a New Jersey bakery; Thornhill was carrying mail, Gawler driving a cab, and Shenton working for his father's maintenance company.

"The good ones are still there," said Lester. "If you take 30 guys, and 12 of them can play football, you're doing a good job. If you get 15 to 18, that's high. Yes, you can make mistakes on players. To get 60 who can play football, you need four exceptional years.

"It takes five years' recruiting to have a good football team. We didn't have time. Hell, Knute Rockne couldn't have recruited enough players to win with the time we had. I know that not one of those guys was mistreated. They might think so, but they always got the benefit of the doubt."

Indeed, the only player anyone thought was run off was the smallish Kostelnik, who quit under Claiborne and transferred to Slippery Rock. "I got hurt a lot, but I didn't think I got run off," says Kostelnik.

Bob Abbott and Ed Serembus quit the same moment of the same morning 10 days before the 1972 season. They had been lagging throughout practice and an assistant told them that if they didn't want to do the grass drills they could leave. They left, after jogging to Claiborne and shaking his hand.

"He wanted us to sign away our scholarships," says Abbott. "He kind of said he'd make things bad for us if we didn't. I told him I didn't want to sign without talking with my dad." But both signed away their aid before they left the room.

A great deal of Abbott's athletic life had been spent working toward becoming a pro football player, and he admits the adjustment to academics was not easy. Abbott had withdrawn from school in June 1972, and with the help of the athletic department had been reinstated a month later. After he quit again, in December 1972, it took him five months to be reinstated.

"If I had it to do over again, I would go to an established football school, with a tradition and a coach who has been there for a while," he says. Abbott, Lane, and Brian Dominic later confined their football activity at Maryland to an intramural team called "The Grateful Dead."

But Serembus had second thoughts about quitting, despite outstanding grades. "That 3.2 wasn't enough," he says. "I wanted to be a player. Three months after I quit I asked him [Claiborne] if he'd take me back. He said he'd leave it up to the players and they voted me back on the team. I earned my scholarship back during winter workouts and spring practice."

Kehoe says the athletic department has a higher rate of retention and graduates than the school as a whole. He adds that "workships" (jobs on campus or within the athletic department) are available for players whose eligibility has expired but who are shy the necessary credits to graduate.

"Ideally, you don't want any dropouts, but that's not always possible," says Claiborne. Of the 32 players in Lester's third—and last—recruiting class, 26 still were active under Claiborne.

Obviously, Claiborne reaped the dividends of Lester's recruiting. Those last Lester classes included several players who helped Maryland to the Peach Bowl in 1973 and the Liberty Bowl in 1974.

"Face it, everybody bitches," says Romano. "When you lose, somebody listens. When you win, nobody seems to listen."

Neville says the best way would be for a player to pay his

way through college. "That way you're more your own boss," he says. "That way if you wanted to quit you wouldn't feel as bad. And if you stayed you'd feel even better."

But would any of the players tolerate all that work and all that pain and still pay for his education? Very few say yes.

13 / The NCAA:
Official Policeman

THE NATIONAL COLLEGIATE ATHLETIC ASSOCIATION SERVES as the governing body for the athletic programs of 669 member institutions of higher learning. And, if some of those schools also are fortunate enough to land a Joe Namath here, a Bill Walton there, change that to institutions of higher earning. The more so-called blue-chip players a school lands, the better the prospects for bowl or post-season tournament appearances and all those luscious gate receipts and abundant television money that goes with them.

Because the competition for high-caliber athletes is so fierce, the NCAA, formed in 1906, has enacted more rules than Robert to control that hectic, tempting, at times nasty but above all fascinating game called recruiting.

"Rules, rules, rules. It seems like there are 18 million rules," says Louisville basketball coach Denny Crum. "You can't help but violate a few. It's so easy to get fouled up."

Indeed, the current NCAA manual contains 51 pages of single-spaced bylaws. The recruiting section covers 10 of those pages, runs some 4,500 words, and is broken down into 8 section headings and 29 official interpretations.

In the back of the 253-page manual there are 209 "cases" involving hypothetical situations that may crop up, and the answers to solving those messy sorts of problems, when a school is courting a potential Pete Maravich, a future Oscar Robertson.

For example:

"Situation: A prospective student athlete visits a member institution's campus, during which time he is provided with a date.

"Question: Is it permissible for the institution to provide entertainment expenses for the prospect's date?

"Answer: No. A member institution shall limit entertainment during a campus visit to the prospective student athlete and his parents (or legal guardians)."

Basically, the NCAA allows member institutions to offer student athletes no more than a scholarship for room, board, tuition, books, and laboratory equipment, plus $15 a month for incidentals. The $15 has been in effect since 1957. So much for inflation.

A school may pay legitimate expenses for a prospect to make one campus visit which may last only 48 hours. The youngster must be put up in a dormitory or comparable living quarters on campus, and he must be given meals comparable to those offered to undergraduate students on campus. The visit also must take place during the athlete's senior year in high school.

College coaches and other recruiters may visit a prospect as many times as they wish at any location off campus, but they are not allowed to pay for the athlete's transportation to any meeting place, or spend any money entertaining or feeding him off campus. The rules prohibit the school from providing a prospect the use of a car on his visit.

Still, according to Warren Brown, the NCAA's head investigator, and his assistant, Bill Hunt, the rules apparently are not deterring a number of America's college coaches from cheating on a grand scale.

Brown is a 34-year-old air force veteran. He is a serious fellow who weighs the consequences of every word he speaks. Hunt, his assistant, is a bit more easygoing. He is 32, with a law degree from SMU and several years' experience as a sportswriter with the Corpus Christi *Caller.* There are also two more full-time investigators: Dave Berst, a former baseball coach and dean of admissions at Mac-Murray College in Jacksonville, Illinois, and Lynn Nance, a former FBI investigator.

Through the summer of 1974 the four were working on approximately 25 active cases, with 30 to 40 cases in the preliminary stages and a total list of 65 schools either under investigation or scheduled to be investigated over the next 12 months.

Brown's office technically is under the NCAA's Infractions Committee, though he admits he has almost complete autonomy—and an unlimited budget—to pursue investigations at his own discretion. And, at its August 1974 convention, the NCAA Council, in a major breakthrough, voted to add another eight investigators to Brown's staff, one for each NCAA district, and the full membership was expected to approve the additions in January.

The length of NCAA punishment varies according to the severity of the violation. Occasionally, if a school breaks a rule unintentionally, a mere private reprimand or censure is issued and never released to the public or press.

From the time its investigatory arm was established in 1952, until 1969, the last year for which full records are available, there were 115 cases of schools disciplined by the NCAA. Since then there have been about 35 more.

"Recruiting," says NCAA executive director Walter Byers, "gives us more problems than anything else."

There have been all manner of juicy collegiate scandals over the past 50 years, one of the most intriguing involving a UCLA fullback allegedly named Clois (Shorty) Key, who played for two seasons under his brother's name, Ted Key, in the 1930s. UCLA turned itself in on that one, and Key was ruled ineligible on the eve of an important game against California. It was learned that Key had been admitted to UCLA as R. F. (Ted) Key from Panhandle High School in Texas. Key never attended Panhandle. He was barred from college football by the NCAA, and spent 15 years as a professional wrestler.

In 1956 the Pacific Coast Conference was broken up after it was learned that USC, UCLA, California, and Washington were paying athletes more than the conference allowed for expenses. It all started when two Washington players became disenchanted with football coach Jon Cherberg, who in turn said his authority had been undermined by R. C. (Torchy) Torrance, the proprietor of a slush fund augmented by $28,000 in revenue from a professional game held in Husky Stadium.

George Stephenson, a former California football player who also played for UCLA, told the Oakland *Tribune* that he and nearly the entire UCLA team had received $40 a month each from an office in Westwood. He confessed, he said, "to get the whole mess straightened out now that Washington has started."

USC became involved when a Los Angeles housewife, active in education projects, became suspicious when a politician listed as a member of the Southern California

Education Foundation evaded her offers to help the organization as a volunteer.

She contacted the Internal Revenue Service, where educational foundations must file financial statements, and asked about the 40 names shown on the report as having been helped by the foundation. "Lady," the IRS clerk told her, "you are looking at the roster of the USC football squad."

Her husband, a UCLA supporter bemoaning the penalties levied against his school over Stephenson's allegations, told UCLA officials about the USC fund. An investigation directed by Deputy District Attorney J. Miller Leavy, a Bruin alumnus himself, substantiated the story. Forty-two members of the Southern Cal football team had been receiving $45 a month from the slush fund.

All four schools were placed on probation. UCLA was barred from the Rose Bowl for three years, USC and Washington for two. USC, UCLA, and California were ordered to pay $50,000 in fines, and $180,000 was impounded from their share of Rose Bowl receipts. The loss of income from television appearances was $150,000 to $200,000 per school.

In 1961 the University of Colorado football team won the Big Eight championship and a trip to the Orange Bowl. The following year, it was learned that boosters had built up a slush fund to pay players with coach Sonny Grandelius' blessing. Thirty-seven players in all were banned either by the Big Eight or the NCAA; the university fired the coach; and Colorado was placed on three years' probation.

Over the last 15 years many other big-name schools have been penalized severely: Indiana for football recruiting violations, Illinois for a $21,000 slush fund that cost football coach Pete Elliott and basketball coach Harry Combes their jobs, Florida State twice for basketball infractions, and on and on.

In November 1972 Southwestern Louisiana was told by the NCAA that it had investigated complaints of violations and "found them to be of sufficient substance and reliability to warrant an official inquiry."

The NCAA sent a list of charges to the university, asking school authorities for a response. The school received a temporary restraining order to allow it further time to answer the NCAA's allegations. Normally, the NCAA's official public statement after a school has been punished lists violations only. No names. During the course of court proceedings, however, the charges were made public and printed in full by the Lake Charles (Louisiana) *American Press.*

According to the NCAA, the school was guilty of falsifying test scores, paying monthly salaries (center Roy Ebron was to earn $450 a month), providing cash loans before and after students enrolled, allowing payoffs for outstanding performances (Dwight Lamar allegedly earned $100 from an alumnus for his play against Oral Roberts one night in 1971), and supplying free clothes, free cars, and free airline tickets.

"They were guilty of just about every rule in the book," says Hunt. "I don't think we've ever seen anything quite like it, and I hope we never will again."

In 1973 Southwestern Louisiana received "by far the most serious penalty ever handed down by the NCAA," according to Hunt, following a two-year investigation of the Lafayette, Louisiana, school. Guilty of more than 140 violations in its basketball program, Southwestern was placed on indefinite probation in all sports for four years until 1977, at which time the athletic program will be reviewed for possible reinstatement.

The school also was stripped of all voting privileges and committee memberships in the NCAA. Southwestern will not be able to appear in any NCAA-sponsored television games, nor will it be allowed to compete in any post-season or tournament matches for the duration of the probation. But the worst blow was the NCAA's insistence that the school drop its basketball program until August 3, 1975.

On January 6, 1974, another scandal was made public. The NCAA, in what it called "one of the most serious" cases it had ever considered, placed Long Beach State on probation for at least three years, citing 26 violations of bylaws governing football and basketball recruiting.

The charges reportedly were based on 74 investigative points. Two days later, basketball starters Roscoe Pondexter and Glenn McDonald were ruled ineligible for the 1973–74 season. While on probation, the school will be unable to participate in post-season play or appear in any NCAA-sponsored television games, in all sports.

"When we investigate," says the NCAA's Brown, "we talk to everyone involved. We don't have the authority to make people talk to us. You just have to have a certain amount of mental toughness for this line of work. We have no legal authority, and that hurts us."

"We go wherever the action is," says Hunt. "Have you ever watched Columbo? Well, we're not that smart, but we do take that relaxed approach. We just keep asking, and saying thank you. We just keep going and going and going until we get it."

Jerry Tarkanian, the former Long Beach State basketball coach, who left the school for Nevada-Las Vegas before the NCAA took its action, charged that the NCAA did not dig deep enough. "The NCAA has really done a job on me," he said after the penalties on his old school were announced. "Several of the alleged violatons stem from the NCAA taking the word of a bitter player who flunked out of school. I denied the statement but the NCAA took the kid's word without any evidence whatsoever.

"They'll take the word of anybody. If they want to talk to any disgruntled athlete for any reason, they will. And if the kid lies and they believe him, you have no recourse. You're at their mercy.

"Oh, God, it's a joke, a joke. We were raped at Long Beach. I was so much cleaner than those other guys that it hurts. . . . The whole thing is so unfair that it has drained me emotionally and mentally. I can't sleep nights. . . . I've always loved the college game, but this has soured me."

Of the 74 charges leveled against Long Beach State, 6 were general reprimands, 9 involved free lodging for athletes, and 13 covered free transportation. Of the remaining 46, the football and basketball programs each were charged with 23 violations.

Among the football violations were charges that linebacker Charles Lewis received credits for courses he never took or classes he never attended; that a booster lent large sums of money to athletes and helped pay off loans owed by student athletes; that All-America running back Leon Burns was given as much as $275 a month to assist him in paying the rent, and his wife, Diahan, was provided a job as an inducement to his enrolling at the school; that another booster, a wealthy realtor and a former president of the school's touchdown club, cosigned a $500 promissory note for Jim Kirby, a running back.

Lewis, the linebacker, told Ray Kennedy of *Sports Illustrated* that "when I got back to San Francisco City College and decided to stay and get my JC [junior college] degree, Miller [Bill Miller, an assistant coach] and Coach [Jim] Strangeland flew in from Long Beach and cracked up a deal right there at the airport.

"If I signed, I wouldn't have to go to school at Long Beach the first semester, just come for spring practice and they would take care of the grades. So I signed. They were buying me and they were buying grades.

". . . when I came down for spring practice, I moved in with Russ Guiver. Man, he had some crib. I had my own bedroom with a color TV and everything.

"Russ used to drive his Lincoln to practice every day and he always brought along his little black checkbook. The most I ever hit him for was $50 because I was mellow with the dude. After I enrolled, Miller gave me a telephone credit card number to use and I had a job as a janitor at the Student Union for $120 a month, but most of the time I wasn't there."

Kirby, the running back, told Kennedy that he received $50 a touchdown and $1 a yard from Long Beach State friends and alumni. He had a $250-a-month job and never paid rent in the three years he lived in Long Beach. "I took a pay cut coming to IBM," he said.

Violations against the basketball program included 14 involving fraudulent test scores, as well as improper tryouts of prospective players, expense-paid trips to games for ineligible team members, and a charge that Tarkanian told Eugene Short, a high school All-America from Mississippi, that his family would be moved to Long Beach and that a job would be found for his mother if he enrolled.

Tarkanian has denied all the charges. "It's unreal, unreal," he told Kennedy. "We started with nothing. I took the trouble kids that nobody else wanted, figuring that I could help them and they could help me. But if you buy a kid, you can't coach him. There were problems, sure. . . . But a lot of those kids got some pride and dignity, learned about responsibility and commitment. . . ."

"There is no doubt in my mind," replied Hunt, "that

Tarkanian was guilty of all the things we said he was. It was an absolutely thorough investigation. He did what we said he did, and it's that simple."

Hunt and Brown prefer not to discuss individual cases at length, if at all, nor will Arthur Bergstrom, now the NCAA comptroller. He ran the NCAA's investigations almost singlehanded from 1954 until Brown took over in 1970.

Bergstrom, in fact, refuses to answer any questions dealing with schools or highly recruited athletes because "there's no sense dredging up people's past sins. It would just hurt them again unnecessarily. I won't talk about any individual cases." So much for two decades of recruiting history.

"We have all kinds of violations," Brown says, "but to me, the most flagrant ones occur when an institution adjusts academic statistics, like changing grades to get kids in, or eligible. Some schools arrange to have substitutes take the entrance examinations, or change the high school transcript around."

Southwestern Louisiana was accused of those very deeds in the case of Roy Ebron, its 6-foot-8 center who now toils for the Utah Stars in the American Basketball Association.

"Student-athlete Roy Ebron," the NCAA charged, "was certified eligible as a freshman during the 1970–71 academic year on the basis of a fraudulent ACT score of 20 which was not actually attained by the young man. . . . In light of Ebron's D grades in high school, ACT section scores of 19 in English, 23 in math, 20 on social sciences, and 10 in natural sciences appears to be a unique if not an impossible accomplishment. [A score of 20 on an ACT exam is considered above average.] Ebron's SAT score [his College Boards] was 481 [out of 1600]. Based upon the Chase Barrett Table of Concordance, a 20 ACT score is equivalent to a 924 SAT score, a little less than twice the SAT score Ebron actually attained."

The NCAA also provided at least one witness who saw Ebron in his dormitory room on the day and at the time the ACT test was being administered. Ebron's signature, a witness claimed, did not match the one scrawled on his alleged test paper.

"We've also had kids enrolled in junior colleges and the kids didn't even know about it," says Brown. "The kid never registers or enrolls, he never goes to classes. But he gets credit and can transfer to the four-year school in good standing. To me, these kinds of violations are far more severe than giving a kid money or a car, although we certainly don't condone that. But academics is what it's all about. That's why there's an NCAA. These are supposed to be students."

How does Brown and his staff decide which school they will investigate? Often, schools will turn each other in when they believe they have been illegally outhustled for a prize recruit. "We get tips from informants to whom we promise anonymity," says Brown. The NCAA also uses published stories in the news media as well as reports from coaches, parents, and recruits who have had particularly troublesome experiences.

Last year, for the first time, Brown and his staff interviewed most of the recognized blue-chip senior football and basketball athletes, questioning them about tactics used to recruit them.

"We hear 90 per cent of all the rumors, too," says Hunt. "A lot of them are wrong. Coaches have a tendency to say 'I didn't lose him, they just bought him.' A lot of it you have trouble substantiating. The kids we talk to, though—it's amazing how much they cooperate. We've got a lot of honest people out there. I think a lot of these kids get insulted when coaches try and buy them.

"But I also think a lot of the stuff is exaggerated. One reason we have all these rumors—well, it's like when we were kids, all the boys had to talk about the girls they had scored with, how fast their cars went, that kind of thing. If you didn't do it, you told stories.

"Well, you can now toss a lot of these so-called violations in that category. A kid will tell another kid he got $100 from a certain school when he visited there, or he'll tell him they promised him a car. It just builds up.

"But don't get me wrong. There are people cheating out there. We pretty much know who they are, and when they give us eight more investigators, nobody's going to be able to get away with anything.

"But I know a hell of a lot of coaches are upset about this whole recruiting thing. I tell you, if I was a coach I'd be damned if I could buy players and still go home to the wife and kids."

Hunt, Brown, and many other NCAA types say they are heartened by recent efforts of many coaches to clean up recruiting problems before the situation creates major scandals in college athletics. At its March 1974 convention in Greensboro, North Carolina, the National Association of Basketball Coaches presented a series of 15 recommendations to the NCAA for possible future consideration.

A recruiting committee set up by the coaches conducted a survey of 25 recently graduated college players who were highly recruited in high school, 25 current high school stars, 25 sets of parents of such athletes, and 25 athletic directors at major basketball colleges. They found that more than one-eighth of the 229 schools playing major-college basketball—as many as 30 institutions—were making illegal offers to prospects. The study also indicated that all the cheating schools offered cash, that 80 per cent offered cars, and half offered clothing. "Forty per cent of all the youngsters interviewed were offered illegal inducements," said Frank Arnold, the committee chairman and an assistant coach at UCLA.

Among the coaches' recommendations were proposals that a potential student-athlete not be contacted by a school until after his junior year; that the NCAA provide condensed recruiting guides for member conferences; and that prospects be required to sign only one letter-of-intent starting at 8 A.M. on May 1 each year.

There are now two different types of letters-of-intent, or letters a prospect signs committing himself to a certain school. If a youngster signs a conference letter-of-intent with, for example, Tennessee, he may not attend any other school in Tennessee's conference, the Southeastern. However, he can still sign with any other school in the country. Once a student signs a national letter-of-intent, he must attend the particular school he has chosen. Most coaches would prefer to have only one letter-of-intent, the national.

The coaches also called on the NCAA to penalize guilty parties "up to and including ineligibility to participate in NCAA-sanctioned games. Guilt would attach to staff members as well as players."

They recommended that guilty staff members be prohibited from active recruiting of prospective athletes and that institutions involved in rules infractions be subject to stiff—with "stiff" underlined—monetary fines by the NCAA. The NCAA does not actually impose fines now, though a school can be ordered to return funds and trophies gained through participation in championship events.

The proposed rules also emphasize that innocent parties —other members of the team or staff not involved in the violations—should not be penalized. Under such guidelines, the University of Oklahoma could not have suspended quarterback Kerry Jackson for the 1973 football season. Nor would Oklahoma have had to forfeit eight of its games in the 1972 season because an assistant coach allegedly changed grades on a high school transcript to allow Jackson to enter the school.

If Jackson knew nothing of the altered transcript, as the university suggested when it blew the whistle on itself in mid-April 1972, and he had acceptable academic standing in college, why then should he have lost a year of eligibility and his teammates suffered the consequences of his not being available as their quarterback?

The question must also be asked in the Long Beach State case. Though most of the violations involved basketball coach Tarkanian, he had left the school before the NCAA imposed its sanctions and had already coached at the University of Nevada–Las Vegas for the 1972–73 season. Nevada–Las Vegas was not placed on any sort of probation, and Tarkanian suffered no penalty for his transgressions at Long Beach State.

The NCAA took a first step toward amending that inequity when its council, in August 1974, voted to recommend that future sanctions be directed only against an individual player, coach, or staff member if it can be determined that no other team member participated in the violation. The full membership also was expected to approve the change at the January convention.

In 1974 another major recruiting reform came from a rather unlikely source—the University of Texas in Austin. Darrell Royal, the Texas athletic director and football coach, occasionally used to fly prospects over to The Ranch on the Pedernales to meet his good friend, Lyndon Johnson, and maybe even convince the president to throw a barbecue in honor of a good ol' boy who also happened to be a 6-foot-3, 250-pound whale of a defensive tackle. But lately, Royal says, he has become appalled by the tactics some of his distinguished colleagues have been employing. "I'm more concerned about it than ever before," said Royal. "I used to think everybody exaggerated it. But we've had too many people come here and tell us what people have offered them. That's hard to swallow."

So Royal, the Texas athletic director, offered to contribute $5,000 to start a war chest that the NCAA could use to beef up its investigations staff and clean up the whole sordid mess. Other officials said they, too, would like to contribute to such a fund.

Brown admitted the NCAA could use the cash and all the additional help, but added, "Recruiting can't be controlled by rules. Legislating won't do it. It will take a real effort by the coaches to clean it up. Whether or not they do it is another story. There's an awful lot of competition to win, and those kinds of pressures stimulate enough of them to cheat."

Still, a good many coaches take the attitude of South Carolina basketball coach Frank McGuire. "Most of the time I don't want to know what goes on," he says. "When a prize recruit comes in here, he's shown around by Mr. So-and-So, a prominent businessman. Whatever happens, happens on that end."

"Personally," says Bob James, the Atlantic Coast Conference commissioner and chairman of the NCAA's recruiting committee, "I don't think you can legislate morality. It's that simple. Some of these rules help, but until the coaches decide they're not going to stand for it, nothing will get better."

"I think recruiting violations get worse and worse and worse every year," says Louisville's Crum. "I can name you a half-dozen of the worst cheaters I know right off the bat, and everyone knows who they are and knows they're cheating. Basically, it's money under the table. It's the one thing they can give to the kids they can't check on. You give cash, it can't be traced."

Hunt, meanwhile, says the NCAA is handling approximately the same number of cases each year, so very little has changed. "As soon as we get those extra eight guys, though, we'll be able to smoke. Right now, nobody can base their whole program on cheating and not get caught. But with eight more we'll be able to jump on a situation instantly, within a week, a month at the most. It's going to make it tougher than hell to cheat."

Tom McMillen, Maryland's All-America and a Rhodes scholar in 1974, would also prefer to see the NCAA become more actively involved in educating the high school athletes. "Kids just don't know the kinds of schools they should go to," McMillen says. "It's too bad the NCAA can't prepare a detached, objective analysis of every school in the country, list all the different departments, describe the environment of the campus, talk about the athletic facilities, the number of All-Americas the school has produced." Nothing like McMillen's "Consumer Reports" now exists for the gifted athlete.

In 1974 the NCAA produced its first recruiting handbook for high school students. It is considerably simpler than the NCAA manual the colleges have to cope with. "The manual," says LSU's Dale Brown, "gives you all that stuff, but you need a constitutional lawyer to figure out what the hell they're saying."

There have been other, far more serious charges leveled against the NCAA and its enforcement arm. "A lot of rules," says Marquette's Al McGuire, "are obsolete and not realistic, especially for the poor black kids. A lot of times I wonder, Where does the ghetto black athlete even get a suitcase to go anywhere? What do you do when a kid needs a pair of pants? What do you do when a kid's mother is sick, 1,500 miles away, and he's at your school only because he plays basketball? How does the kid get home?"

One former Long Beach assistant coach even implies that race was a major factor in the NCAA's investigation of his school. "I think every player they talked to on the basketball team was black," he says. "Go back and look through the years what the NCAA has done. They slap down every school that is challenging the big powers. Louisiana Tech and Southwestern Louisiana were taking over for Louisiana State. Western Kentucky had knocked off Kentucky. Florida State had replaced all the schools down there. New Mexico State had replaced New Mexico. Long Beach was bucking USC. All the new powers were using black players. . . . It was said that every school in the country recruiting black kids from out of its area had to pay their air fare because their parents couldn't buy the tickets. A school like Long Beach had no money so we had to use a credit card, and the NCAA found out about it. Wealthy schools can pay cash out of their pockets . . . or get alumni to do it."

"It's a ridiculous charge," counters Warren Brown. "We don't care about the color of a person, only if the facts are there."

"If anyone thinks the Long Beach case occurred in a vacuum," says Hunt, "they're not looking around. They haven't talked to the people at California-Berkeley, Oklahoma, Western Kentucky, New Mexico State, Pan American, Cornell, Southwestern Louisiana, North Carolina State, Centenary, Louisiana Tech [schools that have been placed on probation in the last three years].

"Our procedure just doesn't work to 'get' any school. If something is wrong, we don't care who it is; we try to take care of it. Look at the schools that are on probation or just have been. They're not all gypsy merchants, not all small or big, well-known or less known, with great athletic traditions or with no athletic traditions. The facts simply indicate otherwise."

The facts also indicate that unless the cheating stops, the NCAA will have a far more serious dilemma on its hands than the betting scandals that rocked the sport in 1951.

14 / Big Decisions

IN HIS HEART, Bruce Buckley had known for months that he would accept an athletic scholarship to North Carolina, although he allowed several other colleges the chance to convince him otherwise. Adrian Dantley's decision was more complex, with four different schools at four different times capturing his affection before he signed with that perennial recruiting winner—Notre Dame.

Both players were shielded, whenever possible, by their high school coaches, and both were counseled by mothers full of trust and patience. Dantley was more actively hustled because at least one top tout, Howard Garfinkel, considered the De Matha forward among the best high school players he had ever seen.

In varying degrees, Buckley and Dantley saw America's most talented collegiate basketball coaches at their best and also their most vulnerable moments. Buckley insists his experience was "pleasant and uneventful, really." Dantley says he received "about four" illegal offers.

Carolina began seriously courting the 6-foot-8 Buckley in July 1972, after his junior year at Bladensburg High, and all but assured his signing with a visit to the Chapel Hill campus in the fall.

"I can't imagine anyone topping that weekend," he said later, and no one did. He was quartered in the posh Carolina Inn on campus and escorted by at least one member of the basketball team wherever he went. He sat behind the Carolina bench when the Tar Heels played the Chilean basketball team and had a 50-yard view of the Virginia-Carolina football game. He also was treated to a Seals and Crofts concert.

"I was never alone," he said. "What I really liked about the trip was the spontaneous organization. There was never a timetable, but everything went so smoothly. I never felt like I was imposing. The players were candid, and they seemed so natural to me."

The summer before his senior year Buckley and his mother visited the University of Virginia with a group of a dozen other basketball prospects and their families. But Virginia assistant Chip Connors scouted him on an off-night early in Buckley's senior year and then—apparently unimpressed—simply stopped calling.

Duke coach Bucky Waters made a strong pitch. As an assistant to Vic Bubas in 1960, he had recruited Jay Buckley. But Bruce never took a recruiting trip to Duke. He had been there countless times to watch Jay play and did not feel the school and campus had changed significantly.

He also was concerned with newspaper stories indicating Waters might not last much longer at the Durham, North Carolina, school, as well as reports of disgruntled players who had either transferred or quit the team.

Through most of his senior year, Buckley even had mild doubts about Carolina—"a matter of confidence," he said, "not being sure I could play in the ACC."

So he kept his options open at William & Mary of the Southern Conference and also listened to George Washington University's pitch, just in case he wanted to stay closer to home. But his confidence soared in a few post-season all-star games—and so did Carolina's, "because I like their style. It's intelligent basketball. Five or six passes before somebody takes a good shot. It's a system where everybody shares and contributes, even the guys on the bench."

Buckley never considered academic lightweights, because "I wanted to go to a school with a strong scholastic tradition. The most difficult part about it was telling coach Waters I wasn't coming to Duke. He said he couldn't understand how I made my choice without visiting, and I couldn't really give him any good reasons why I didn't.

"He made me feel kind of guilty, but when you think about it, I shouldn't have to feel that way. I never signed a contract to see Duke. I really don't think I owed him anything but 'No, thank you.' I respect Dean Smith so much. He told me he was only interested in five or six people in the country, and I was one of them. I was honored."

Smith was so certain of the commitment that he waited 10 days after Buckley called and said he would enroll at Carolina before formally signing him. Time usually is vital in signing a prospect, as American University discovered with a prospect named Glenn Price.

Price had told then-coach Tom Young that he would attend AU, and the school thought the decision important enough to hold a press conference the next day. Most schools go through the legal formalities of signing a player as quickly as possible, then stage it later for reporters. AU's affair was attended by everyone it invited except Price, who balked and later enrolled at St. Bonaventure.

But the day after Easter, Dean Smith arrived at the Buckleys' apartment, had Bruce sign conference and national letters-of-intent, then sat down to a ham and potato salad dinner before heading back home.

Dantley's recruitment was anything but smooth, although neither he nor his family seem permanently scarred by the experience. He eliminated North Carolina for one of the reasons that appealed to Buckley and was most frustrated and depressed with the recruiters for their lack of dignity.

Dantley received letters of inquiry from an estimated 250 schools, among them Stout State, Point Park, Panhandle State, Carson-Newman, and dozens of others he barely knew existed. He seriously considered about 25, and by March 1973 had whittled that number to a manageable 8, a figure that remained constant for nearly two months although the names changed now and then.

Dantley was at the stage in the decision-making process where confusion was rapidly pulling away from reason, where a dozen schools had compelling attractions and a dozen coaches were beginning to pressure him for a choice.

"I'm not going to Minnesota—no, maybe I'll go there," he said at one point. A few minutes later he made a similar remark about Marquette. The schools he discussed were:

Minnesota: Although he was confident he could start as a freshman at any school, this one seemed the easiest because the top seven players had departed. A member of the Big Ten was attractive because its rules allowed more physical contact, and Bill Musselman impressed him as a dedicated coach.

Indiana: Another Big Ten contender on which he could

be the dominant offensive player backed by two unselfish guards.

North Carolina: An Atlantic Coast Conference power under one of the country's most respected coaches, Dean Smith. He might not get the publicity there he would at another school, but a former Tar Heel, Robert McAdoo, had recently signed a pro contract for an estimated $1 million.

North Carolina State: Of all the schools he considered, this one seemed to have the best chance of winning the NCAA championship. (In fact, it did.) As with all the southern schools he considered, though, there was doubt about whether a young black could be happy.

Maryland: Only a few minutes from De Matha and one of the favorites from the beginning. He had received "a ton" of mail from alumni, according to his coach, Morgan Wootten, and the guard-forward position recently vacated by a gifted redhead named Jim O'Brien after three years seemed to be searching for a Dantley-like player.

Southern California: It had a certain glitter, but UCLA was in its league and he did not like the idea of entering each season with two almost-certain losses.

Marquette: A power under cagey Al McGuire. But Dantley thought the coach might be tempted by a pro offer, and leave within four years. He had rejected UCLA because there were indications John Wooden might retire within four years.

Notre Dame: A contender the first week in March that actually seemed to be losing ground. Dantley was concerned that the two guards, Dwight Clay and Gary Brokaw, might be reluctant to pass up shots and that when they did the ball would go immediately to center John Shumate. In addition, the Notre Dame coach, Digger Phelps, was rumored to be signing every prospect in sight. "I'm getting selfish," Dantley said. "I want to go somewhere I can shoot."

Nevada–Las Vegas: Undoubtedly the next major-college power under new coach Jerry Tarkanian, formerly of Long Beach State.

Hawaii: Like Nevada–Las Vegas, he considered it for all the obvious reasons. He then rejected these two schools and Southern California because they were much too far from home.

Florida: The major reason he considered it was assistant coach Terry Truax, a former De Matha aide and close friend of the family. Of all the recruiters, Truax probably was Mrs. Dantley's favorite. Still, it was another southern school.

Cincinnati: A contender because of assistant Aubrey Nash, former De Matha standout in football and basketball who helped introduce Dantley to playground-style play. In addition, the school had an excellent reputation among black players.

Smith and Carolina led the Dantley chase the longest— throughout his sophomore and junior years—the coach having once gone out of his way to fly to Washington to watch a De Matha practice before joining his team for a tournament in San Francisco.

The day after Dantley won honors as the most valuable player in the Dapper Dan tournament Smith flew to Washington on the same plane and later drove the family home. He lost Dantley that afternoon. Smith rarely loses on the court or in the living room, yet Dantley got the impression the coach considered him "lazy."

"He was telling me I was lazy on the fast break, that after I threw the pass I walked to half court," Dantley said later. "I thought he was wrong. I also thought they substituted too much. I still think he's a great coach. It was just one of those things."

At that point, the first week in April, North Carolina State and coach Norm Sloan had assumed the lead, Sloan having taken a 7 A.M. flight from Raleigh to Washington the morning after State won the ACC tournament to watch Dantley play.

"It's really a close-knit team," Dantley said. "And the team and the town are, too. I was afraid it wouldn't be like that in the South.

"I know David Thompson would get all the publicity, but I'd get some," he continued. "Then maybe he'd leave early [for the pros] on a hardship case, and I'd be the man. I want to go somewhere that when there's not much time left and they need a basket they go to me."

Fifteen shots a game, not counting offensive rebounds, seemed a reasonable goal to Dantley, and he thought he could realize that at State despite the gifted Thompson and giant Tom Burleson in contention for the ball.

After a month, though, State began to lose some of its appeal. But none of the others were able to leap into a firm lead. Not even the dynamic Driesell.

The Maryland coach had captured Dantley's mother. "I like Lefty," she said time and again. Yet for all his skills and countless hours of attention over a three-year period, Driesell could never sustain the lead.

Whenever Dantley would announce a list of schools, it mostly read: Minnesota, North Carolina State, *and* Maryland, or Notre Dame, Minnesota, *and* Maryland. The closest the Terrapins apparently came to landing Dantley was when his coach, Morgan Wootten, considered an assistant's position under Driesell.

By mid-April, Dantley seemed thoroughly frustrated. The phone kept ringing and names and questions kept dancing about in his mind. Driesell and Sloan, Musselman and Knight. . . . Big Ten or ACC? . . . Will I get the shots? . . . Who's the best coach? . . . When will it all end? A host of other gifted shooters, runners, throwers, and jumpers in this and other years all faced the same dilemma.

"I always wanted to go to USC, but my grades weren't good enough to get in without some junior-college work," said O. J. Simpson. "Yes, I was offered money by some schools, but I'd rather not name names. Yes, there were famous people trying to influence me. Willie Mays wanted me to go to Utah, I think."

"My father had heart trouble, and when my older brother went away to school at Kansas he was very disappointed," said Wes Unseld of the Washington Bullets. "While I was being recruited he suffered a mild heart attack. I thought it might give him pleasure to see me play, so I picked Louisville, my hometown school.

"The best offer I ever had came about in a strange way. I was told by one coach to stay at home one night because I'd be getting five phone calls. That night, five different businessmen each offered me $100 a week—that's right, $500 a week—if I went to that school. I don't know if they would have come through because I never went there."

"I didn't start playing basketball until late in high school, about my senior year," said Bill Russell, whose San Francisco team held the NCAA record for consecutive victories (60) until the Walton Gang broke it. "I only got one offer of a scholarship, to San Francisco, and I took it."

"No, I wasn't declared a state asset," said the Lakers' Jerry West, a native West Virginian. "That was Rod Thorn. But there were some offers you wouldn't believe."

"I was absolutely determined I was not going through the hassle, so I turned everybody but two schools off after my sophomore year in high school," said Jerry Lucas. "I knew I was going to stay in Ohio, so the only two schools I considered were Cincinnati and Ohio State. Cincinnati gave me the All-America treatment, how I'd do athletically. Ohio State sold me on academics. Cincinnati just used the wrong methods."

Still, all of this was not lifting any of the weight from Adrian Dantley's broad shoulders. Finally, when he seemed at his most confused state, Wootten offered to help break the logjam. Wootten says he had never interfered before that point with any of his numerous college prospects because he did not want to be accused later of influencing a decision.

During and after dinner at Wootten's one night, the Dantleys listed what Adrian wanted in a college—exposure, academics, playing time, etc.—and which colleges best fulfilled them. A point was given for the leader in each category, and at the end of the night Minnesota had accumulated seven points, North Carolina State and Maryland four each.

That seemed to clinch it. Minnesota was the first school Dantley had visited, Musselman impressed him as an extremely dedicated coach, and the Big Ten seemed ideal for his physical style of play. In addition, the Gophers usually drew 23,000 fans to each home game, 18,000 of them in the arena and another 5,000 for closed-circuit telecasts, and the school easily met his academic requirements.

"If I had to make a decision right now," he said one night while watching a Knick-Celtics NBA playoff game on television, "it would be Minnesota." He had visited just two other schools at that point—N.C. State and Maryland—but the word quickly began to filter around the country that Adrian Dantley was about to become a Gopher.

The Dantley-Minnesota rumors immediately triggered what Wootten, a veteran observer of many recruiting battles, termed "the most vicious case of bad-mouthing I've ever seen."

The attacks generally centered on Musselman's "Jekyll and Hyde" personality and an incident at Ohio State a year earlier that had caused two Gopher players to be suspended for the remainder of the season for dirty play.

At first Dantley tended to dismiss the talk, allowing as how he was not without some Jekyll-Hyde traits, either. Gradually, though, his mother began to notice a change.

"They've been very successful," she said on May 10. "At first we'd say, 'Who's saying this, what's the source?' and nobody would say who or what. I don't think that's fair to tell someone something on the basis of rumor. But it's so universal. I'd really rather they'd offer money, because we'd know how to deal with that. They have instilled doubts in his mind. Minnesota is fading."

The day Dantley arrived for a scheduled two-day visit at one school the coach greeted him with "I'll tell you one thing right now—don't go to Minnesota." Dantley left the next morning.

As Minnesota was fading, Notre Dame began—quietly but surely—to move toward the leaders. Dantley had visited South Bend, Indiana, the first week in May, and by May 20 the Irish had pulled ahead.

"I'm leaning toward there now," he said. "I always did like Notre Dame. Fact is I used to dream about it, because of the Knute Rockne movies, I guess."

Then Dantley listed all the positive factors: the chance for national exposure, the challenge of an exceedingly difficult schedule (UCLA home and away on consecutive weekends in January), his mother being able to watch him on television five times and able to travel to see him in person in Madison Square Garden and Philadelphia.

"And the coach [Digger Phelps] is the only one keeping his cool," he said. "The coaches knock each other, act like little boys sometimes when you get down to it. Right now, though, I say I'm leaning toward Notre Dame and they can't say anything bad about it. But I'm not gonna sign yet. I don't have that gut feeling yet."

Dantley had eliminated North Carolina State, Florida, Indiana, and Southern California, however, and was committed to just one more visit—his ninth in all—to the University of Cincinnati.

It was at this late point that Dantley began to be pestered by anonymous late-night phone calls. "Guys who won't identify themselves will call and say, 'Wait a while, something's going to come into the picture.' Then they hang up. I don't even know how they got our number."

At 3 A.M. one day, Virginia Dantley beat her son to the telephone. She recalls the following dialogue:

"Is Adrian there?"

"Why? Don't you know it's 3 A.M.?"

"Well, you see, out here in South Bend it's just midnight."

Mrs. Dantley was somewhat shaken by the call, but she says it did not take long to realize that the call was not from South Bend.

As May ended and June was nearly a week old, when nearly all the other gifted prospects in the country had selected their schools, Dantley finally was about to say no to Maryland and Minnesota.

"I almost signed at Maryland," he said on the day he publicly said no to the school. "It's a good school and Lefty's a good coach, but I don't think we'd get along."

For two summers Dantley had often gone to Maryland and run up and down the Byrd Stadium steps to keep in shape. "One day I stopped and looked around," he said. "I asked myself, 'Do I really want to go here? Naw.'"

So Maryland was eliminated, and, within a week, so were Minnesota and Cincinnati.

Dantley was impressed with Cincinnati "because they do a lot for black athletes," but that attraction, and the lure of Aubrey Nash, were not strong enough. He did not believe all the anti-Minnesota talk, Dantley said, but two former players did not give Musselman a strong recommendation.

For contrast, Dantley had been impressed with the picture his Washington friends Sid Catlett, Austin Carr, Collis Jones, and Bob Whitmore painted of their alma mater, Notre Dame. It seemed yet another illustration of that basic sales—and recruiting—maxim of the most convincing pitch coming from a satisfied customer. Especially from Whitmore, who had experienced the recruiting hassle nearly a decade before, captained the basketball team, earned a degree in economics at Notre Dame, and would return to law school there in the fall.

One school had offered Whitmore $2,000 to sign and $2,000 once he arrived on campus, to be supplemented by $95 a week and perhaps even use of a car. He refused, saying: "It wasn't worth $4,000 for me to ruin my life. Just like they could buy you, they could also sell you. They'll drop you like a scorched potato if you don't produce. They just wanted that flesh, they just wanted that basketball player."

"Notre Dame is the only place where the people didn't knock the other schools and the coach didn't bug me," Dantley said. "I said at the start of the year that the coach that bugs me least will probably get ahead. And the social life at Notre Dame, which I thought wasn't so good, is all right."

And so at midafternoon on June 16—and with the very pen that Catlett, Carr, and Jones had used—Adrian Dantley, who is not Catholic, signed a grant-in-aid to attend Notre Dame. Then he looked backward for a moment, and then ahead.

"Every school I ever visited seemed to be in the lead at one time," he said. "Everybody said to get it over with, but I wouldn't until I was sure. I handled the pressure better than anybody."

During a press conference at De Matha, Dantley was asked if he thought he would be a varsity starter as a freshman at Notre Dame, which had all five starters returning from its National Invitation Tournament runner-up team. Immediately, he said: "Yes, I will."

Modesty was not one of Dantley's strong points. He had said more than once that he considered himself the best high school player in the country and that "no one can handle me one-on-one." Yet these seemed more statements of fact from a candid young man who indeed had outplayed most of his peers than the distortion of self-image that recruiting encourages.

"Now I start everything again," he said of his future at Notre Dame. And the recruiters began chasing another prospect in another town.

15 / Dantley and Buckley: Freshmen

THE TRANSITION, as a student and as an athlete, had been difficult for Adrian Dantley. He left home for the first extended period of his life in September 1973 and arrived at the college of his choice—Notre Dame—not on a velvet carpet but just one of a thousand freshmen.

Most of what Dantley achieves, in the classroom and on the basketball court, comes from hard work, and his first few months away from Washington, D.C., in Middle America, were lonely and frustrating, when he felt his most significant achievement the next four years might not be fulfilling his dream of making All-America but simply passing his first physics course.

In time, during that freshman year, Dantley learned to tolerate Mr. Newton, if not to love him, and became a reasonably strict vegetarian; he played a significant, if not starring, role in the game that ended the longest winning streak in collegiate basketball history and spurned a feeler to turn pro after averaging 18.3 points and 9.7 rebounds for a team among the five best in the country. And, in that most ironic of developments, one of the nation's most highly recruited players became a spirited recruiter himself.

Dantley's problems in adjusting from De Matha High in Hyattsville, Maryland, to the university on the south bend of the St. Joseph river were no different from those of thousands of other freshmen in dozens of other schools— except for one vital fact.

While most of the others could devote full time to their studies and discover diversions to ease the jolt of leaving home for the first time, Dantley was obsessed with winning a starting position on a team that had come within one off-balance shot of winning the National Invitation Tournament the year before.

It may shock some to learn that Notre Dame requires its athletes to read and write, to carry at least a C average to compete. In fact, coach Digger Phelps not only preaches that grades are as important as points but also excuses his basketball players from practice for academic conflicts. Phelps and others kept insisting Dantley get in shape, mentally and physically, but he balked for a dangerously long time.

"Basically, I'm a shy person, and I was scared at first," he admitted not long before the UCLA upset. The reflection came in his single room in one of the oldest dorms on campus, Fisher Hall, hardly the lap of luxury with its cream-colored, concrete-block decor. Literally, he could barely keep the walls at arm's length.

"Everyone told me to go and talk to the teachers, to show enthusiasm, but I thought they might say, 'He don't want to work, he's a ball player.' The other guys [the five other freshman basketball recruits] could go, but I couldn't. Coach told me to miss practices, but at that time I didn't have a starting spot, so most times I'd go to practice instead of seeing the tutor."

Dantley said Bob Whitmore, the former De Matha and Notre Dame standout then enrolled in law school at Notre Dame, and Phelps were the major reasons for his academic and athletic turnabout—Whitmore because of his calm assurances and Phelps because of his not-so-gentle pushes.

"He [Phelps] kept saying, 'You got to want it, we can't do it for you,' " Dantley said. "I'd say, 'Yeah, yeah,' but I was looking away, not in their eyes like I do when I'm serious. I'd look at the floor. Then I got scared. I thought I might fail right out of this place. I missed 10 or 15 practices the first semester and was late for some others. I actually forgot about basketball sometimes, the first time that ever happened in my life.

"At practice the first two or three weeks, I couldn't do anything. I was overweight, about 235, and we'd run, run, run and then run some more. Then we'd scrimmage. I'd be exhausted."

Dantley's concerns in Indiana were evident in his mother's phone bills in Southwest Washington, which averaged about $150 per month. Often he would say he could not imagine things being more bleak, only to phone the next night and insist they were. It was an expensive pattern that continued until the night when his first breathless words were: "Ma, guess what. I passed physics. I got a C."

As Dantley's academic fog began to lift (he averaged 2.2 on a 4.0 system his freshman year), his basketball status also improved. The pounds decreased, his speed and confidence increased, and Phelps announced to the team two days before the season opener against Valparaiso that Dantley would start at one of the forwards.

Dantley broke into a veteran, though young, lineup that included two eventual No. 1 choices in the NBA draft,

6-foot-9 center John Shumate and scoring guard Gary Brokaw; a steady defensive specialist, Gary Novak, at the other forward; and an icy-nerved point guard named Dwight Clay, who had a flair for important last-second baskets in important Irish victories. There was adequate bench strength in freshmen Billy Paterno and Ray Martin.

Ultimately the Irish would win 26 of their 29 games, but their lack of overall height and a schedule as rugged as any in the country did not seem to rate them much chance of replacing UCLA, however briefly, at the top of the national polls.

And so when Phelps' third Notre Dame team opened at home in the huge Athletic and Convocation Center, sometimes called "Austin Carr Coliseum" because that gifted Washington native was its first basketball standout, and won by 50 points there was no country-wide stir.

The wire services pecked out a lead that said "Freshman forward Adrian Dantley led the Irish with 16 points," but this easily could have been 24 or 26 points had a good case of first-game jitters not caused him to miss several relatively easy layups.

Then the Irish beat Ohio State, Indiana, and Kentucky on the road, and, with top-ranked UCLA defeating Maryland and North Carolina State, the pollsters moved them to the second spot in both wire-service rankings.

By then Dantley was averaging 11 shots, 17.2 points, and 9 rebounds, and although he was playing farther from the basket than he had at De Matha, he had won over some skeptics of his ability to shun the soloist's role by taking 34 charges in 9 games. He was able to state confidently that "out of all the high school senior basketball players last year, I made the best decision on a college."

"I'm playing well on a team basis," he said two nights before the UCLA game. "I could have gone somewhere else and averaged 30 points on a losing team. But I think the pros would rather have a winner who scored less."

Outwardly, he seemed to be taking the UCLA pressure rather nicely, although inside his nerves were going at fast-break tempo.

"I think the key to the game is my reaction to it," he said. "The other guys have played them before, I'm just a freshman. The Ohio State game was the biggest before this, because they have crowds of about 18,000. That night I didn't want the basketball or anything. But Shumate taught me some things that night; I calmed down and came along good the second half. That was a turning point."

Dantley said he and Shumate expected to challenge All-America Bill Walton, bothered recently by a bad back, by taking him hard to the basket instead of pulling up short and taking "baby jumpers." It was the sort of aggressive, give-no-quarter style that had been a Dantley trademark for years.

"I'll be ready," he kept telling friends—and himself. "There are a lot of jealous people who don't believe I'm doing so well. They'll judge me by the UCLA game. I dream about the game a lot. How will I feel? How will I react?" He said the dreams moved along smoothly until the game became close. Then he kept waking up.

Reality was better than the dreams, with Dantley making an important steal and layup when the game became close in the final two minutes, and if he had tried to pinch himself just to make sure Notre Dame really had beaten UCLA, 71-70, it would have been nearly impossible to locate an inch of flesh that was not being patted or fondled or hoisted onto the shoulders of a sea of Irish fanatics.

Three weeks after their football team had become national champions with a dramatic victory over Alabama in the Sugar Bowl, and less than 24 hours after their hockey team had whipped top-ranked Michigan Tech, the Irish also were atop the collegiate basketball polls after overcoming an 11-point deficit in about three minutes against a team among the greatest ever assembled.

In the end, the court where UCLA had last lost, on January 23, 1971, and where it had established what was at the time the longest winning streak in collegiate basketball history—61 games in 1973—was awash with the very fans who would not have given their team a prayer of a chance for victory a few minutes earlier.

To be sure, the ghosts of Gipp and Rockne—and other unseen powers—seemed at work as the usually poised Bruins melted amid the thunder of 11,343 voices and the pressure of a team that used three freshmen at times.

Dantley, who had contributed 9 points, 8 rebounds, and 2 assists to one of the most satisfying Notre Dame victories ever, was even more certain that a young black man with no deep religious persuasion could build a solid reputation at this small Catholic school in Indiana.

But the euphoria, as well as the unbeaten status and top spot in the polls, was gone within the week for the Irish. In Los Angeles UCLA gained its revenge, by 19 points, and that night Dantley seemed sluggish and at times intimidated by Walton. He was not even the best freshman on the court, a distinction earned by the Bruins' newest starter, Marcus Johnson.

There was a reason for Dantley's decline, and it had been taking shape for weeks. Mentally he was being drained by his new academic challenge and the added pressure of maintaining his high athletic reputation at a school where a gifted player seemed to pop up behind every sycamore. To compound this, his sensitive nature had been pricked by several fans—and friends—who told him that he appeared fat on television.

So, in an effort to improve his TV image for the second UCLA game, unknown to everyone but himself, Dantley went on a crash diet. In addition, he tried to quickly melt off a few pounds by applying more heat than necessary during his whirlpool treatments. It was not inspired thinking under the best of circumstances, let alone during that part of the schedule that had the Irish averaging a game every two days. And the inevitable came to pass in the second half of the DePaul game January 31. During a time out, Dantley collapsed on the bench from dehydration.

The initial scare was much greater than the illness, though, and Dantley missed just one game. And out of the experience came better and more rigid eating habits, although Dantley took some extreme measures by eliminating most meats from his diet as well as pies, cakes, and his former favorite, pecan rolls. By the summer of his sophomore year, he could accurately be called sleek.

On the court, Dantley also perked up, and he reached a zenith against West Virginia February 23, in another televised game, by scoring 41 points. Nearly everything he shot went in, nearly every loose ball bounced his way, and he left the game to a standing ovation. That night he kept his usual date—with his tutor.

During the latter part of the season, a recruiter from the American Basketball Association quietly approached him and discussed the possibility of his declaring himself a hardship case and turning pro. Dantley said no, firmly, and asked the man to please not bother his mother with the subject, either. The man approached Virginia Dantley anyway, and got another quick no.

Dantley and the Irish moved smoothly—and unbeaten— through 12 games after the UCLA defeat and thought there was no one capable of keeping them from the final round of four teams in the NCAA tournament in Greensboro, North Carolina. It developed that there was—themselves. After a regular-season-ending loss at Dayton, the Irish blitzed Austin Peay in the first round of the NCAA playoffs, then lost to Michigan in the regional semifinals.

Overconfidence was as good an excuse as any, because many of the players had been rooting for Michigan to win the Big Ten title from Indiana, since they regarded the Wolverines as the easier opposition. Dantley had just 2 points that night and took the loss personally. He recovered with 29 points during the consolation-game victory against Vanderbilt.

Generally, Dantley either matched or exceeded every goal he set for himself as a freshman. He felt certain he would start and average about 10 points and 10 rebounds; he averaged 18.3 points and 9.7 rebounds. Significantly, he averaged just 12 shots per game.

But a team must restock its talent nearly every year, especially one that loses a Shumate and a Brokaw to the pros, and players hustled and hassled by recruiters one year must themselves become recruiters the next. Adrian Dantley batted just .500 in his first role as a recruiter. He helped convince an excellent Washington guard, Donald (Duck) Williams, to attend Notre Dame but could not convince an excellent Washington forward, Kenny Carr, not to attend North Carolina State.

The summer before his sophomore year was occupied with three economics courses at Notre Dame and maintaining his skills alone and against other gifted players on the playgrounds. There was time for a brief look backward and a long look ahead.

Adrian and Virginia Dantley had forgotten nearly all but

the pleasant moments of the recruiting experience of the year before. They knew they could have allowed it to take on the circus-like atmosphere surrounding Moses Malone—and so many others—and were most grateful they had not.

"I've been very satisfied with his choice," Mrs. Dantley said. "I can see where he's matured. I think he's helped the school and the school's really helped him. Looking back, it was not difficult for me to stay out of the recruiting as much as I did, because I could see Adrian was doing all the right things. I enjoyed it. He had something to offer them [the recruiters] and they in turn had something to offer him. It was just a matter of making a choice."

The sour taste that remained with the Dantleys was the bad-mouthing of Minnesota when Adrian all but decided to become a Gopher—all the sly slurs directed toward coach Bill Musselman and the confident predictions that the school soon would be on probation. In fact, Minnesota was not placed on probation and had an excellent recruiting year in 1974.

A year after he was accepted at Notre Dame, Dantley saw himself as more disciplined and less likely to make brash statements, having been shown by word and deed that a Notre Dame man should allow his skills to do the talking. Still, his outwardly confident nature was not totally dimmed. Having made honorable mention All-America and been judged the best visiting player to perform in Madison Square Garden by New York media, he considered himself "the No. 1 freshman in the country."

With Shumate, Brokaw, and Novak gone, Notre Dame would be looking directly toward sophomore Dantley for leadership. He reacted to this probable burden with hours of work on moves under the unyielding Washington sun, often causing stares and snickers by strolling through the

Department of Agriculture toward his mother's desk wearing a sweat suit and ankle weights and dribbling a basketball.

Given his mid-season collapse and other problems, it might reasonably be argued that Dantley was a prime example of a freshman, no matter how gifted, being unable to quickly adjust to the transition from high school to immediate varsity status in college. On reflection, he thought the ordeal prepared him better for the dominant role he envisioned as a sophomore. At De Matha, he had anticipated being on a college team that would look to him for the critical plays, direct the ball his way when one shot meant victory or defeat. He would be in such a position his second year among the glories and the ghosts of Notre Dame.

The future did not seem so bright for Bruce Buckley. He chose his college, North Carolina, for reasons beyond basketball and he did not expect to start as a freshman. Still, after his first season yielded a 3.8 grade-point average and 1.1 scoring average, there was the very real possibility that he, like the majority of others before and after him throughout the nation, would find his greatest athletic success behind him.

Healthy and 6-foot-8, a scholar-athlete of distinction at Bladensburg, Maryland, High, Buckley found himself so deep on the bench at talent-rich Carolina that he saw action in just seven varsity games and was not included on the 14-man traveling squad for the Atlantic Coast Conference tournament in nearby Greensboro.

When he returned home after his freshman year, Buckley found even casual friends asking if he was going to transfer to a school where he could play regularly. But he was not one to break a contract easily, even though his roommate,

James Smith, had transferred to Florida State. Logically, he thought that the year's layoff required of transfers would be about the same as two years of learning and varsity inactivity at Carolina.

"It's no heartbreak," he said, "because I didn't allow myself that much expectation. I was prepared for the worst, looking for the medium and hoping for the best. I don't know yet how I feel, really. I'll have to wait until I'm a senior and look back, see what's happened."

When Buckley arrived at Carolina, he discovered Bobby Jones, Ed Stahl, and Mitch Kupchak firmly established in the two front-court positions for which his skills seemed best suited. And he also found that coach Dean Smith had lured two other exceptional tall freshmen, 6-10 Tommy LaGarde and 6-11 Jeff Crompton. If he could recall once being self-conscious about his height at times, he soon realized that three more inches would be useful now.

For most of the first two months, though, Buckley was encouraged because injuries to a few players allowed him to practice with the varsity, which had been his minimum goal as a freshman. And his academic transition was one smooth step from Bladensburg. He had scored 1300 on his College Boards, received credit at Carolina for one math course and a year of language, and was placed in the advanced English course. Then the basketball season began, and with it almost continual uncertainty for Buckley.

"I felt a little like a Ping Pong ball," he recalled. "Every day it was sorta like, 'Well, am I going to get a phone call that says I'm going to practice with these guys [the junior varsity] or am I going to dress for the varsity game or not?' There was some indecision all season, because he [Smith] was juggling 18 or 19 guys. Some days I would practice three days in a row with the varsity, and then I wouldn't practice with them for a long time.

"I couldn't get my feet on the ground. On the JV, I was supposed to be the big rebounder, take it up inside strong. With the varsity, I couldn't do that. I'd try it the first couple of times because I'd been used to JV competition, and Kupchak and Stahl would block the shots. Then I'd have to adjust and worry about boxing my man out and getting all the loose balls I could."

If his academic experience at Carolina seemed the logical progression forward from high school, life with the junior varsity basketball program seemed a trip backward, to Bladensburg-like competition. Yet, with five scholarship players at times, the Carolina JV lost several games it should have won. Part of the reason, Buckley admits, was the ego jolt to players no longer the best at their school not caring to play their best against inferior opposition.

Buckley was not easily recognized on campus, because he tended to travel in tall company anyway, but did not mind the sudden lack of attention. In fact, he was glad his friend on the school paper never got time to produce an often-discussed profile, because he had done nothing he either especially wanted to discuss or thought others would care to read.

Not that his athletic life at Carolina was completely devoid of satisfying moments. He scored the 100th and 101st points against Vermont, and, from the free-throw line, joined the fans in smiles and good cheer—not because yet another Carolina foe had been soundly whipped but because these were his first varsity points.

There were a few other bit parts in varsity performances, including the final few minutes against Clemson when Stahl, Jones, and Kupchak fouled out, although most of Buckley's fondest moments came in the relative anonymity of junior varsity games or practice.

"What is satisfying?" he said near the end of the season, when he was listening to his teammates play in the ACC tournament from his room in Chapel Hill. "Sometimes just a comment that's really sincere from coach Smith at practice is pretty good. If he notices something and compliments me, that can make the entire practice a whole lot easier."

In high school Buckley had detested any of the reserves not giving their best at all times, and now he was in the position of pushing himself to help the varsity by not relaxing and giving the first-stringers honest opposition.

"Once the first team was practicing on its zone defense and every time Ed Stahl would come at me in the corner he'd leave the baseline open," he said. "One time I just exploded down the baseline and got any easy layup. Coach Smith yelled at the first string for a while. That may have messed up practice a bit, but I felt that alone helped the team as much as anything I could do because it showed them they weren't doing it right."

Buckley insisted he "didn't want a whole lot of glory out of JV games because they're just sorta something you do to prime yourself for the varsity." Still, he did score 39 points against a team that escapes memory and scored the final points of a preliminary game forced to be decided by sudden death because the varsity affair was being televised.

"William & Mary said I could play there," Buckley said during one reflective moment. "And I thought about that a lot. But I also thought about the Blue team here, that the five or six second-stringers here are assured of being in every game for a couple minutes. The decision was whether to play a lot, or be in a situation I liked." He chose the situation he liked; he did not make the Blue team.

Even though his roommate decided to transfer, Buckley

did not seriously consider such action "because it's a pretty drastic step, the way I look at it, even though it's not betraying a trust. Things are not that bad.

"If I had been disappointed academically or with the campus life—because basketball was just all right—then I might have decided to stick closer to home. But the academics and the school are real nice, the guys on the team, the weather, everything else is super almost." Everything, of course, except for the nagging notion that he is on a basketball scholarship, after all, and is certain he could have mustered more than 8 points, 5 field-goal tries, 8 free-throw tries, 5 rebounds, and 2 assists for several other varsity programs as a freshman.

"What I would have done differently," he said of recruiting a year later, "is to have visited more places. I actually visited only four schools, and I should have visited maybe Florida, a school in the Southeastern Conference, and maybe one or two more. I'm still convinced the decision I made was the right one, compared to the schools I visited. If it were compared to 20 other schools, it would be 20 times the right one."

As a student, Buckley still is nearly straight-A and leaning toward math, or possibly ecology, although he admits he has yet to discover a teacher as stimulating as Smith, one of basketball's few genuine innovators in addition to being one of its best and most persistent recruiters.

"I can see how his system is right, even though I haven't had a part in it," Buckley said. Yet he admitted, in the summer of '74, having left the Washington area as one of its most heralded players, that he was returning with some doubts about his ability. No longer was he as confident against players he had bested before, or the unknowns who would swagger onto the courts.

And the playgrounds were not necessarily the best place to hone his skills for another assault on the Carolina varsity as a sophomore. These essentially are one-on-one sessions, and the last thing Dean Smith encourages is a soloist.

"What the heck," he said one midsummer morning. "I can stick it out. If I can improve myself, then I'll get to play. If I can't, I'll just try and help everybody else." And wait for the phone to ring.

16 / What Should Be Done

"THE SITUATION IS FRUSTRATING. It may be like blowing sand in the desert. I know some coaches who couldn't stop cheating if they wanted to, because their alumni wouldn't let them." The speaker was Bill Wall, head basketball coach at MacMurray College and former president of the National Association of Basketball Coaches.

"I leave with a warning that you get the NCAA to come down hard on recruiting cheaters. Otherwise, we'll have a major scandal again." The speaker was Jack Rohan, who resigned as Columbia's basketball coach in 1974.

"The pressure to win is a hell of a lot more than just hiring and firing a coach. It's keeping your whole program going. Recruiting is a justified pursuit, without question. Let me put it another way: It's a necessary evil." The speaker was Don Canham, athletic director at Michigan.

"It's a national disgrace." The speaker was Maurice Mitchell, chancellor of the University of Denver.

Educators nationwide are becoming increasingly concerned with the widespread abuses in the field of recruiting. Words like scandal, crisis, and national shame flow freely from the typewriters of America's sportswriters and columnists. The American Council on Education, in the first major study on college sports conducted since 1929, has recommended that a national commission be formed to look into the role of sports on America's college campuses and, hopefully, recommend major reforms.

"External competition from professional sports, selective treatment by the media, pressure from alumni and public have all combined to put big-time collegiate athletic programs into competition with each other not only on the playing field but in the market for entertainers/performers/athletes," the initial report stated. "The need to win on the field has thus led to those ethical problems in the recruiting, financial subsidy, and on-campus care and feeding of college athletes."

George Hanford, who directed the ACE study, listed some of the violations which came to the attention of his inquiry team. They included:

Altering high school academic transcripts.

Threatening to bomb the home of a high school principal who refused to alter a transcript.

Changing admissions test scores.

Having substitutes, including assistant coaches, take admissions tests.

Offering jobs to parents or other relatives of a prospect.

Promising one package of financial aid and delivering another.

Firing from a state job the father of a prospect who enrolled at a university other than the state team's.

Tipping or otherwise paying athletes who perform particularly well on a given occasion and then on subsequent ones.

Providing a community college basketball star with a private apartment and car.

Getting grades for athletes in courses they never attended.

Enrolling big-time university athletes in junior colleges out of season and getting them grades there for courses they never attended.

Using federal work-study funds to pay athletes for questionable or nonexistent jobs.

Getting a portion of work-study funds paid to athletes kicked back into the athletic department kitty.

"The existence of such violations is admitted by those involved in intercollegiate sports and documented in press reports and the files of the several national associations and athletic conferences," Hanford wrote. "The admissions, however, never relate to the campus or the conference or region of the admittee. It is always another coach, another president's institution, another conference, or another region that is guilty. Conceivably, the alumni or booster club could be doing something unethical, but no one in authority 'on our campus' is aware of them."

Hanford went out of his way not to make any specific references to solutions to the many problems his group explored, saying that would be the function of the national commission. But even a cursory reading of his findings suggests that unless the cheating stops, college sports cannot survive as we know them today.

That also is beginning to dawn on many of the coaches and athletic administrators around the country, as well.

Abe Lemons, the wisecracking Pan-American basketball coach, suggests that all cheating will stop when each coach is given $25,000 and allowed to keep whatever he doesn't spend on recruiting.

Lefty Driesell and several other coaches have, half-seriously, advocated a high school draft, similar to the professional draft. "I don't know how you'd do it," says Driesell, "but it's worth thinking about." Not really, because a draft would be a blatant violation of a student's freedom of choice.

Marquette's Al McGuire maintains that until coaches get long-term security, in the form of multiyear contracts or tenure, the cheaters will never, as he put it, "get rubbed out." But tenure seems a good way off for the coaches of America for all the obvious reasons. Young coaches get older, and so do their ideas. And if a coach knows he has lifetime security, why bother to bother?

Universities can replace their coaches and assign them to other duties, but can they afford to keep one loser, and maybe even three or four, on the payroll? Hardly.

"Faculty criticism of excessive professionalism in intercollegiate athletics has rent some programs asunder," reads a faculty athletic committee report at the University of North Carolina. "But we could find no evidence of successful faculty intervention to protect a humane and compassionate coach against an adverse won-and-lost record in this or any other conference. An ominous silence appears to be the rule rather than the exception."

Former Notre Dame basketball coach Johnny Dee suggests eliminating paid visits to the campus by recruits.

"If they're getting $16,000 educations paid for, they can afford to pay their own way. What about the poor kid who can't afford the trip? Well, what's wrong with him going to school close to home?"

Chuck Dekeado, a former Southern Cal recruiter, would like to see agents assigned to prize recruits. "Their job," he said, "would be to evaluate whether it's really worth a kid's while to choose one school over another."

Then, of course, there are the extreme solutions. One would base all financial aid on need, not athletic ability. In 1973 a proposal was presented to the NCAA membership that would do just that.

"Two reasons among others," Hanford wrote, "were advanced in support of the proposal. One, it is standard practice with respect to virtually all other students. This argument makes good sense, particularly to those who decry special treatment of athletes. . . . Two, it saves money.

"With two such compelling arguments on its side, why was the proposal rejected? It was turned down in 1973 and 1974 (by NCAA membership) because the big-time inter-collegiate athletic establishment on balance doesn't trust itself.

"The argument was that such a policy would generate even more under-the-table payments than now exist. Note not only the admission that they now exist, but also the opinions that the pressure to win is so great that coaches would exceed the need formula and that athletes would accept such awards."

Still, the eight-member Ivy League now comes closest to the need-only scholarship policy, and it seems to work reasonably well. "We simply don't have athletic scholar-ships," says Andy Geiger, athletic director at Brown. If an athlete applies to more than one Ivy League school, the financial aid directors of the institutions involved consult to determine the amount of money the prospect and his parents must contribute to his education. All the schools, then, make the same offer.

"It's all based on need," says Geiger. "That doesn't mean we don't recruit like hell, though. But nobody in this conference can make a kid a better offer than another member school."

North Carolina State athletic director Willis Casey is firmly opposed to scrapping the present scholarship system. "You ask whether the money we're getting wouldn't be better spent on cancer research. Sure it would," he said. "But so would a lot of other money that's spent for frills in this society.

"We're not the ones who put the emphasis on athletics. It's put there by the Associated Press when they send people out to cover our games. The media is mostly responsible. In an ideal world, I'd like to see us provide coaches for the students here and just teach the boys who come out and want to play. But that was tried before, and it didn't work.

"The scholarship system isn't perfect. We support the idea of awarding them only on the basis of need. But it's still the best system we've been able to come up with."

Not everyone would agree. Perhaps the most radical proposal of all suggests that youngsters merely play for pay once they leave high school. Certainly professional baseball and hockey have no qualms about paying large bonuses and salaries to acne-faced teen-agers, so why should the colleges?

"Make no mistake about it," sayd Michigan's Don Canham. "This is business, big business. Anyone who hasn't figured that out by now is a damned fool."

So why not allow the best players to go to the highest

bidders, draw salaries—over the table—and, if they like, attend an occasional class or two? Maryland's Tom McMillen, a Rhodes scholar, rejects both play-for-free and play-for-pay proposals.

"Promoting professionalism on a university campus is not the answer," he said. "The kids wouldn't stand for it. Why, if I'm a student, should I pay to subsidize a team of professionals representing my school, spending my tuition money?

"The other extreme is no scholarships and financial aid through university procedures. But then a player can say, 'Hell, why should I kill myself on a basketball court and get nothing for it?'

"I do think you've got to keep away from those million-dollar budgets. That's when the almighty dollar enters into it. The old television has done a lot of harm. We played North Carolina State, and the television money that came in from that game was incredible. TV is a problem. It doesn't keep college sports in perspective."

But whose perspective? To the free spenders, that game and all other ballyhooed, nationally televised affairs are magnificent spectacles—what college sports are all about.

To the people at Amherst or Whittier, two schools that have never been on national television, the game probably represents everything that is evil and insidious about college athletics.

And that is precisely the point. Why not simply allow each school to determine its own athletic destiny? Let a school decide the size and scope of its athletic program, whom it chooses to play, what standards its players must meet, and for what price they will play.

The NCAA has been moving in that direction by splitting into three divisions, and the future is likely to produce an even greater gap between colleges obsessed with winning national championships and colleges content to train student-athletes. All of which seems proper enough.

The American Basketball Association showed the major-college basketball powers that they must hike the minimum wage to keep their best players for four years. The World Football League may begin raiding Ohio State, Texas, and the other collegiate football powers to stock some of its weaker franchises.

One fundamental question we pose is whether the NCAA has a useful function beyond keeping records and negotiating television contracts. So many of its rules are impossible to police and so many of its penalties cause too many innocent victims to suffer.

Legislating morality does not seem the answer, nor does increased enforcement. The cheaters will continue to cheat, and not even the entire FBI could root them all out.

Why not let the individual schools work things out for themselves? If they want their stadiums filled and their teams on national television regularly, let them give the athletes cars, $200 a month, and all the New York strips they can devour.

If it takes several thousand dollars to keep a player from becoming totally professional, pay him. Most schools could justify it economically anyway. And most schools operate under an academic double standard now.

It is time for a wave of realism to wash away the hypocrisy in collegiate athletics. Let the recruiters bring their offers above the table, at last. Let them continue to tell the athlete that he means so much to the university. But let him know how much.

17 / The Moses Malone Debacle

THE ONE CASE that emphasized the damn-the-cost zeal of the recruiters, their talents for lifting hypocrisy to unimagined heights, and the need for reform of collegiate athletics was the year-long courtship of a 6-foot-11 C-average student in Petersburg, Virginia, named Moses Malone.

Like Jackie Moreland and Wilt Chamberlain, Jerry Lucas, Kareem Abdul-Jabbar (Lew Alcindor), and Tom McMillen, Moses was regarded not merely as prospect of the year in 1974 but as some superior being capable singlehandedly of leading a school to "The Promised Land."

There even was a special version of The Ten Commandments for this Moses ("Thou shall not drive the lane. . . . Honor thy right and left hand. . . ."), although more than the usual number of academicians considered it something of an outrage that a teen-ager who needed two A's in the final semester of his senior year to lift his scholastic average above C should be coveted by so many colleges.

After he averaged 35 points and 25 rebounds his senior year, and especially after the Utah Stars picked him in the American Basketball Association draft, Malone attracted the usual caravan of hustlers to his doorstep.

Unlike Adrian Dantley and Bruce Buckley, though, Malone, also raised primarily by his mother, had no one either able or willing to keep his recruitment even within the usual chaotic bounds.

There were bulletins drifting about the country almost daily: Houston will find the missing father. . . . Oral Roberts will cure the mother's ulcers. . . . Any school that signs Moses will be on probation. . . . This is recruiting at its worst. The latter was correct.

Recruiters hustled up the ramshackle steps at 241 St. Matthews Street at such a pace that Malone sometimes disappeared for hours. He finally had to set up a code system of knocks (1-2-3-4, then 1-2, then 1-2-3) so he would know when friends were visiting.

One of Moses' closest friends revealed that he once went to the house with a recruiter and knocked in a special way, indicating he was not alone. There was no answer. The friend climbed on top of the porch and looked through the window. There was Moses, all 6 feet 11 inches of him, flat on the floor, hiding.

As the pressures on him mounted, Malone became more and more reluctant to make his feelings public. Reportedly, if a conversation became boring, he simply left the room. Still, newsmen kept yipping at his heels, and newspapers treated his every word as cosmic.

When Malone played in a post-season all-star game at the Capital Centre in Landover, Maryland, all four Maryland coaches and three players were in attendance.

There were places the Maryland players could visit more easily than the Maryland coaches, such as the locker rooms immediately after the game, and Driesell even took a suite on the same floor as the post-game party.

Private moments for the players were rare, but Malone managed a few when he took a side route to the bus after the game. His retreat was through a back room that housed Circus America, and it was the first time elephants and horses had been used as picks.

Maryland spent an estimated $20,000 during its recruitment of Malone, and a New Mexico assistant, John Whisenant, spent three months in a Petersburg motel. Another assistant, an exceedingly active recruiter known to his friends as Pitstop, reportedly once hired a private plane and told the pilot to "fly south, to The Man." Coaches at the schools where Malone could not qualify academically watched enviously from the sidelines.

"I decided that to get Moses to New Mexico I had to work harder and be more dedicated than anyone else," said Whisenant, 30 and single at the time. "I had to be in there fighting when the others were out recruiting somewhere else."

"I've heard of coaches staying three or four days in one place putting the last-minute sales pitch on a kid," said Richmond basketball coach Carl Slone. "Driesell is famous for that. But three months? It's incredible. Everyone's talking about it."

Whisenant had no difficulty justifying his tactics. "If Moses comes to our school," he said, "it will put us in the top two or three in the nation next year." So he moved to Petersburg at the end of March 1974, after New Mexico was eliminated in the NCAA tournament.

During his months in town, Whisenant managed to gain the shy youngster's confidence. "A few times, he's spent hours here hiding from Lefty Driesell and the other coaches," he said. "He watched the NBA playoffs on my motel television. I don't really know why he's accepted me and rejected everyone else. Maybe it was because I got to know him as a person first before I started trying to recruit him. If he hadn't accepted me, I wouldn't have stayed here this long."

Despite his long stay in Petersburg, Whisenant managed to sign three other players, relying primarily on quick flights and the telephone to do his work. In the three months, he spent approximately 10 days in Albuquerque.

Whisenant first became involved with Malone when the All-America visited the New Mexico campus the previous year. Malone was greeted at the Albuquerque airport by the governor, and he was escorted by representatives of the state's two senators when he changed planes at Washington's National Airport for the trip west.

"For us to have a chance, I had to stay here," Whisenant said in June. "It was too expensive to start flying back and forth. Last week Lefty came down here three times. It would have cost us a fortune to do the same thing. We have a great budget. We can have all the money we need, but not quite that much."

Whisenant was in there fighting at the end, after Virginia Commonwealth, Houston, Detroit, Hawaii, and all the others had fallen by the wayside. After Malone had narrowed his choices to three, Whisenant successfully talked him out of signing with Clemson. But he could not keep Malone from signing with Maryland.

At 7:15 A.M. on June 20, 1974, after expense-paid visits to about 20 schools and after dozens of coaches in turn had come to his doorstep, Malone became a Terrapin. According to Petersburg athletic director Bob Kilbourne, Malone still was asleep when Robertnett Hayes, his high school coach, went to his bedroom holding Maryland's letter-of-intent.

"This is Maryland's contract. Would you like to sign?" Hayes asked Malone, according to Kilbourne. "Then Moses rolled over," Kilbourne said, "and his eyes lit up and he got this big smile on his face. Then he signed. Hayes left the room and Malone apparently rolled over and tried to go back to sleep.

"Coach Hayes came downstairs and showed Lefty Driesell Moses' signature," Kilbourne said, "and Lefty jumped up in the air about three or four feet. He went upstairs, hugged Moses and told him, 'You've made me the happiest man in the world.' Moses got up then and they went out to breakfast."

Later the newspapers were dotted with allegations. Witnesses reportedly told NCAA investigators that at least two schools had committed recruiting violations while wooing Malone, and Malone's uncle, Charley Hudgins, was quoted by United Press International as saying representatives from one Southern school twice gave him a "yellow envelope with more than $1,000 in it." He insisted he returned the money each time.

"It is very evident to all that Mr. Hudgins was provided with some money," Atlantic Coast Conference Commissioner Robert James said in late August, "but I can't place it. On a certain date [June 11], he had $1,000 and used it as a down payment. We do know that it was rebated to him."

Whisenant allegedly allowed Malone to drive his car until Petersburg officials put a stop to it. Maryland, Clemson, and New Mexico insisted they had broken no rules while recruiting Malone, and everyone insisted that the 1974 Chrysler Imperial he bought was financed on the up and up.

The Western Athletic Conference saddled New Mexico with some relatively minor restrictions "because we found one recruiter had, on at least one occasion, let him [Malone] use his rental car," said Commissioner Stan Bates in December.

The very day that Malone signed a grant-in-aid with Maryland, the Maryland chancellor, Charles E. Bishop, announced that he was leaving to become president of the University of Arkansas. Interestingly, and perhaps significantly, one Washington newspaper displayed the Malone story across the top of its front page; the story of the chancellor's leaving made page four of an inside section.

But the saga of Moses Malone was to dribble on for another two months, and end with his becoming the first high school player to jump directly to the pros—for a reported $1 million from the Stars.

The Stars told the teen-ager that, for the next few years, he was worth more than not only Maryland's basketball coach and athletic director combined but also every college president in the world.

Basketball, like the presidency, is not one of those callings that require a college degree, although an apprenticeship of sorts seems necessary. Until a few years ago, all was very orderly in the sports world, with the pros allowing the colleges four years to maximize profits on an athlete before they told him for whom he could play and for how much.

Economic pressures have forced the American Basketball Association to upset this tidy arrangement, and the Stars' drafting Malone to bolster their forecourt was the logical extension of a pattern that saw Julius Erving, Jim Chones, and other gifted players turn pro before their collegiate eligibility had expired.

"It was unreal; I doubt anything like it will ever happen again," said Stars coach Bucky Buckwalter of the week-long ordeal to coax Malone into turning pro. "We [himself, Stars

president Jim Collier, and General Manager Arnie Ferrin]
put 932 miles on the car in six days just going between
Petersburg and Washington. The toll road between Richmond and Petersburg used up $19.75 worth of my quarters.

"The sneaking around, the spiriting Malone out back
doors, the driving back and forth—it was all incredible. We
had an outpost on a hill overlooking Malone's house. We'd
drive up there, park the car, check the layout to see who was
around, and then we'd go down.

"Once we had to crawl through the backyard and were
attacked by a big dog. At least I think it was big. When
you're crawling, they all look big."

Predictably, Maryland athletic director Jim Kehoe was
quick to join other collegiate officials in decrying the Stars
for "this gross lack of respect for a high school student."
Presumably Kehoe had been busy dickering over contracts
and dreaming of lucrative television revenue after Malone
agreed to accept Maryland's offer of a free education.

In fact, Malone may have meant as much economically
to Maryland as he does to the Stars, and the frustration for
Terrapin leaders was that the NCAA would not allow them
to bid for his services.

For nearly two years, Malone had the best and most
famous basketball coaches in the country vying for his
signature on a scholarship, even though he would not be
admitted were it not for his postgraduate basketball skills.

"They dragged me to as many as 24 schools," Malone
told *Sports Illustrated.* "Sometimes they brought me in to
meet the president of the university, who talked to me like
he wanted to be my father. That made me laugh. They fixed
me up with dates, then when I got home, those girls would
call me long-distance and pretend they were in love with
me. What kind of stuff is that?"

All along it had seemed that nearly all the advice he

received came only from men with a vested interest in his 6-foot-11 frame, and it hardly was surprising that he became so withdrawn for one whose future seemed so bright. For a young man with a limited educational background, Moses Malone already had learned some valuable lessons.